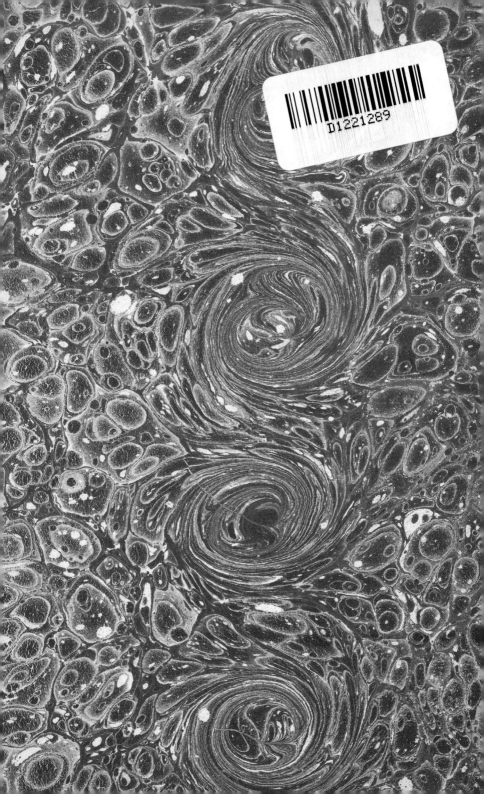

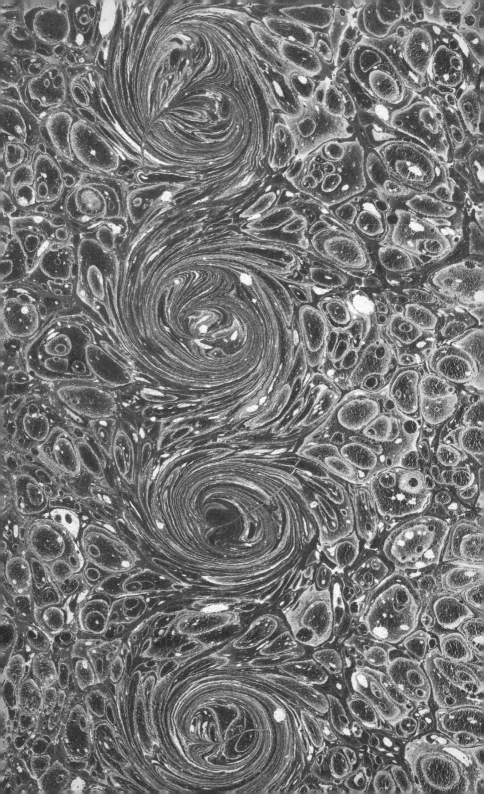

A
SHAKESPEARE
MOTLEY

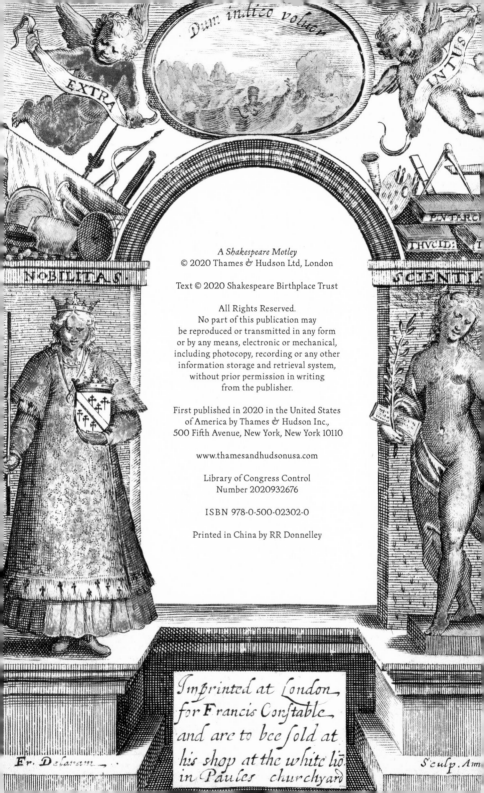

First published in 2020 in the United States
of America by Thames & Hudson Inc.,
500 Fifth Avenue, New York, New York 10110

www.thamesandhudsonusa.com

Library of Congress Control
Number 2020932676

ISBN 978-0-500-02302-0

Printed in China by RR Donnelley

A
SHAKESPEARE
MOTLEY

An Illustrated Compendium

225 illustrations

Shakespeare
birthplace trust

INTRODUCTION

'Here's the book I sought for so'
Julius Caesar

☞ WILLIAM SHAKESPEARE, playwright and poet, was born in Stratford-upon-Avon and baptized on 26 April 1564 at Holy Trinity Church. Married at eighteen to Anne Hathaway, he split his time between writing and the theatre in London, and family life in Stratford-upon-Avon. He died on 23 April 1616 aged fifty-two.

The Shakespeare Birthplace Trust was founded by public subscription in 1847, and today the Trust cares for the five heritage sites associated with Shakespeare in and around Stratford-upon-Avon. It's a measure of Shakespeare's profound impact and enduring legacy that we welcome some three-quarters of a million visitors to Shakespeare's family homes each year.

This book is inspired by these homes, and the stories they tell about the time that Shakespeare lived and worked in, as well as by the wealth of materials in our internationally recognized collections. The idea for a miscellany was informed by the richly illustrated Shakespearean scrapbooks and miscellanies in our archives, compiled in the nineteenth century from earlier sources. In creating our own motley assortment, we have delved extensively into our library of rare printed books from the sixteenth and seventeenth centuries. This collection includes books about nature, gardening

…nd domestic manuals, printed maps, literary translations and numerous works Shakespeare himself would have known and read. All of the illustrations here are taken from our archive, and many inspired the entries we've included. Intriguing, quirky, unusual and beautiful, a number of the images are reproduced for the first time, re-presented in an eye-catching way that we hope will spark interest and make connections for the reader. Often the smallest visual details can be the most illuminating: zooming in on the engraved frontispiece of a medical book, for example, reveals a stuffed alligator hanging from the ceiling of an apothecary's shop just as it is described in *Romeo and Juliet*, and on close inspection a panorama of London Bridge includes the sight of traitors' heads on spikes, and men drowning in the water below.

Written with the general reader in mind, the entries are intended to give a taste of the immediate world Shakespeare knew, and the worlds he imagined in his works. Shakespeare was not writing in isolation but drew on the domestic and the natural world, and the literary and folk cultures of his time. We still recognize in his works universal themes such as love, grief, jealousy and power, but specific references that were common knowledge in Shakespeare's time may be lost to us today, and we hope that this book will restore some of these resonances for the reader, from the tools and techniques of the falconer to the healing properties of spiders' webs.

This assortment is by no means comprehensive, either in the scope of the topics, or within individual subjects themselves. A larger volume might have included, for example, dedicated entries on the four humours, the New World and the imagination, as well as more about the theatre and Shakespeare's own family and fortunes. Nor is the book intended as a traditional reference book. Instead, we hope that the entries serve as jumping-off points into Shakespeare and the period, and that readers might be inspired to find out more, to seek out the original sources, and to read – or return to – Shakespeare's endlessly intriguing poems and plays.

ACTOR

The best actors in the world, either for tragedy, comedy, history, pastoral, pastorical-comical, historical-pastoral, tragical-historical, tragical-comical-historical-pastoral, scene individable or poem unlimited.

☞ SHAKESPEARE was an actor, writer and shareholder in one of the two leading playing companies in London, called The Lord Chamberlain's Men, later the King's Men under the patronage of James I. Shakespeare's fellow actors and shareholders included John Heminges and Henry Condell, who would compile the first complete works of Shakespeare after his death, and Richard Burbage, the leading actor of his day, who played the starring roles in *Hamlet*, *Othello* and *King Lear*.

Along with Shakespeare and the principal 'sharers', the company was made up of hired men and boy apprentices. Plays frequently had more roles than there were players, so actors would often have to double up, playing two or three different roles. Women were not legally permitted on the English stage, so the female roles were played by boys. Cleopatra alludes to this in *Antony and Cleopatra* when, fearful of being ridiculed on stage in Rome, she imagines seeing 'Some squeaking Cleopatra boy my greatness / I'th' posture of a whore' and, in *A Midsummer Night's Dream*, Flute, cast as the heroine in the Mechanicals' play, complains: 'Nay, faith, let me not play a woman. I have a beard coming.'

The Mechanicals are amateur actors, often portrayed for comic effect, but their earnest endeavour to put on a play is also an insight into theatre practice of the time. In their opening scene, Peter Quince gives each actor his lines: 'But masters, here are your parts, and I am to entreat you, request you, and desire you to con them by

Changling   Simpleton

Sᵗ I   Falſtaſe   Hoſtes   Clauſe

French Dancing Mr.

From Kirkman's Drolls.   Publiſhed 1872

The Workes of William Shakespeare,

containing all his Comedies, Histories, and Tragedies: Truely set forth, according to their first ORIGINALL.

The Names of the Principall Actors
in all these Playes.

William Shakespeare.

Richard Burbadge.

John Hemmings.

Augustine Phillips.

William Kempt.

Thomas Poope.

George Bryan.

Henry Condell.

William Slye.

Richard Cowly.

John Lowine.

Samuell Crosse.

Alexander Cooke.

Samuel Gilburne.

Robert Armin.

William Ostler.

Nathan Field.

John Underwood.

Nicholas Tooley.

William Ecclestone.

Joseph Taylor.

Robert Benfield.

Robert Goughe.

Richard Robinson.

Iohn Shancke.

Iohn Rice.

tomorrow night, and meet me in the palace wood a mile without the town by moonlight. There will we rehearse.' Actors learned their lines from rolls of paper containing only their own part and the cue lines from the preceding speeches, written out from the company's playbook. Snug the joiner is keen to have his part straight away, asking Quince: 'Have you the lion's part written? Pray you, if it be, give it me; for I am slow of study.' Rehearsing during their free time in the mornings, professional playing companies would have a new play ready to perform in about two weeks.

In *Hamlet*, the arrival of a company of players at Elsinore affords another view of the actor's craft, when Hamlet advises them how to 'Speak the speech'. He cautions the actors to avoid bellowing and big gestures, and to 'o'erstep not the modesty of nature. For anything so overdone is from the purpose of playing, whose end, both at the first and now, was and is to hold as 'twere the mirror up to nature.'

Whereas Hamlet would have art imitate life, for Shakespeare, life also imitates art. Hearing the news of his wife's death, Macbeth declares: 'Life's but a walking shadow, a poor player / That struts and frets his hour upon the stage, / And then is heard no more.' And in *As You Like It*, Jaques prefaces his speech chronicling the seven ages of man with the declaration:

> *All the world's a stage,*
> *And all the men and women merely players.*
> *They have their exits and their entrances,*
> *And one man in his time plays many parts,*
> *His acts being seven ages.*

As You
Like It
2.7

APOTHECARY

❡ FIRST DESCRIBED in England in the thirteenth century as people who sold wine, spices and herbs from a stall or shop, apothecaries were originally members of the Guild of Pepperers. In 1428, as wholesaling and merchant trading grew, pepperers, apothecaries, grocers and spicers were all incorporated under the Worshipful Company of Grocers. Bucklersbury, a short lane in the heart of London, became home to the newly emerging spicer-apothecaries, and from their shops they prepared and dispensed drugs as well as selling spices, perfumes, confectionery and spiced wines. By Shakespeare's time apothecaries were skilled practitioners and dealt primarily with the sale of drugs, and poisons, for medicinal use, although, with no recognized medical authority or skills, they were not entirely reputable. Under James I, the creation of the Worshipful Society of Apothecaries in 1617 helped to establish the profession formally.

A Medicinal

DISPENSATORY,

Containing

The whole Body of Physick:

DISCOVERING

The Natures, Properties, and Vertues of
Vegetables, *Minerals*, & *Animals*:
The manner of Compounding MEDICAMENTS,
and the way to administer them.

Methodically digested in

FIVE BOOKS

OF

Philosophical and Pharmaceutical

INSTITUTIONS;

THREE BOOKS

OF

PHYSICAL MATERIALS

Galenical and Chymical.

Together with a most Perfect and Absolute

PHARMACOPOEA

OR

Apothecaries Shop.

Accommodated with three useful TABLES.

Composed by the Illustrious RENODÆUS,
Chief Physician to the Monarch of *France*;
And now Englished and Revised,
By *Richard Tomlinson* of London, Apothecary.

LONDON:
Printed by *Jo: Streater* and *Ja: Cottrel*; and are to be sold by *Francis Tyton*,
at the three Daggers in Fleet-street. 1657.

Crols sculpsit.

In Shakespeare's plays apothecaries are mysterious figures, with their drugs and poisons, and the potential effects, being shown as dangerous to dabble in. In *Romeo and Juliet*, Romeo seeks out an apothecary to buy poison, and describes in detail the small shop and the odd assortment of ingredients on the shelves, including animals, skins, seeds and flowers. The apothecary is poor and thin. Misery has 'worn him to the bones' and he is dressed in 'tattered weeds'. Recognizing a man as desperate as he is, Romeo knows that the apothecary will gladly sell him the poison:

> *I do remember an apothecary,*
> *And hereabouts a dwells, which late I noted,*
> *In tattered weeds, with overwhelming brows,*
> *Culling of simples. Meagre were his looks.*
> *Sharp misery had worn him to the bones,*
> *And in his needy shop a tortoise hung,*
> *An alligator stuffed, and other skins*
> *Of ill-shaped fishes; and about his shelves*
> *A beggarly account of empty boxes,*
> *Green earthen pots, bladders, and musty seeds,*
> *Remnants of packthread, and old cakes of roses*
> *Were thinly scattered to make up a show.*
> *Noting this penury, to myself I said*
> *'An if a man did need a poison now,*
> *Whose sale is present death in Mantua,*
> *Here lives a caitiff wretch would sell it him.'*
> *O, this same thought did but forerun my need,*
> *And this same needy man must sell it me.*

Romeo
and Juliet
5.1

APPLE

And sometime lurk
I in a gossip's bowl
In very likeness of
a roasted crab,
And when she drinks,
against her lips I bob,
And on her withered
dewlap pour the ale.
A Midsummer Night's Dream 2.1

❡ A POPULAR, plentiful fruit in Shakespeare's England, apples were also used in cookery and cider-making. The song of winter in *Love's Labour's Lost*, 'When roasted crabs hiss in the bowl', evokes the popular Tudor drink of wassail, a hot spiced ale or cider, served with roasted crab apples, traditionally offered on Twelfth Night. Part of Shakespeare's garden at New Place had been given over to orchard in the sixteenth century, and his plays suggest a familiarity with the techniques of growing and grafting fruit trees. In *Henry IV part 2*, Justice Shallow invites Sir John Falstaff to 'see my orchard, where, in an arbour, we will eat a last year's pippin of mine own grafting', and his guests are presented with a dish of 'leather-coats', a variety of russet apple.

There are other apple references too. In *Twelfth Night*, Malvolio describes the boyish Viola as 'a codling', a name for an immature apple; and, in *Love's Labour's Lost*, Holofernes declares a plump deer as 'ripe as the pomewater' – the pomewater being a 'great whitish apple, full of sap or moisture', according to Shakespeare's contemporary, the apothecary John Parkinson. In *Love's Labour's Lost* we also

14

meet the character of Costard, a fool named after one of England's oldest apple varieties, the custard apple. This name had also become a slang term for the head, hence Sir Hugh's threat in *The Merry Wives of Windsor* to 'knog his urinals about his knave's costard'.

ARMOUR

¶ HENRY VIII had established some of Europe's best armourers in his workshops at Greenwich, London, and the sixteenth century saw the development of armour reach its peak. The design and decoration of armour became increasingly sophisticated, but the musket ball and modern means of combat that relied on infantry rather than mounted cavalry rendered full plate armour obsolete by the end of Queen Elizabeth I's reign. The weight of armour required to withstand a musket shot made it increasingly impractical to wear and, while the traditional knight's full suit of armour was still worn for ceremony and tournaments, only the head and chest protection were retained by the new, fleet-of-foot professional soldier.

Shakespeare's plays span the history of armour, from the Roman Antony as a 'man of steel' in his buckled breastplate, to Benedick

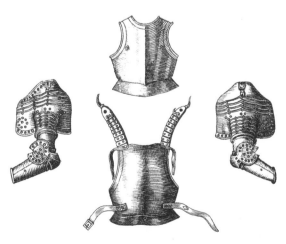

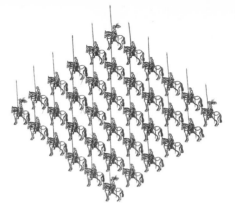

in *Much Ado About Nothing* recollecting when Claudio 'would have walked ten mile afoot to see a good armour'. In *Henry V,* Shakespeare evokes the armourer's craft and the industry of pending war:

Henry V
4.0

> *The armourers, accomplishing the knights,*
> *With busy hammers closing rivets up,*
> *Give dreadful note of preparation.*

And ahead of battle in *Henry IV part 1,* Vernon paints a vivid picture for Hotspur of Prince Hal and his comrades 'All furnished, all in arms, / All plumed like ostriches':

Henry IV
part 1
4.1

> *I saw young Harry with his beaver on,*
> *His cuishes on his thighs, gallantly armed...*

Cuishes and beaver are both types of armour, cuishes being pieces to protect the thighs and the beaver being the helmet's visor. While it might not have been possible to costume whole platoons in full armour for a play, Shakespeare would have been well aware both of how the language of armory enriched the verse, and of the dramatic impact of presenting an actor in armour. In *Hamlet,* the ghost of Hamlet's father appears wearing 'his beaver up'. He is 'Armed at all points exactly, cap-à-pie,' dressed head to toe in a suit of armour. Horatio recalls it is the same armour the king had on 'When he th'ambitious Norway combated'– a portent of war on the one hand, a symbol of a bygone age on the other.

16

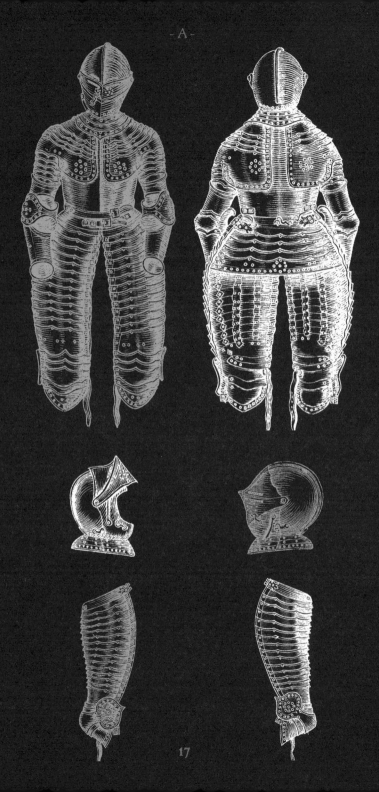

18

BEAR

Or in the night,
imagining some fear,
How easy is a bush
supposed a bear...

A
Midsummer
Night's
Dream
5.1

☞ ACCORDING to Shakespeare's contemporary, Edward Topsell, bears are 'dreadful, fierce,...night ranging...terrible' creatures. A bear appears in *The Winter's Tale*, giving rise to Shakespeare's most famous stage direction, 'Exit, pursued by a bear.' Having abandoned the baby Perdita in the Bohemian wilderness, Antigonus is pursued and reportedly 'torn to pieces with a bear'.

Alongside the theatre, bear-baiting was a popular entertainment in Shakespeare's England. Captive bears were chained to a post and tormented by a pack of dogs. This wretched existence is evoked by Falstaff when he says he is as melancholy 'as a lugged [baited] bear'.

A chained bear is also the symbol of Shakespeare's home county of Warwickshire. The Earl of Warwick alludes to this image in *Henry VI part 2*:

Now by my father's badge, old Neville's crest,
The rampant bear chained to the ragged staff...

Henry VI
part 2
5.1

BEE

A
Midsummer
Night's
Dream
3.1

The honeybags steal from the humble-bees,
And for night tapers crop their waxen thighs...

❡ BEES were revered by the Tudors as providers of food, medicine and light in the form of candles. They were kept in basket-shaped hives called skeps, their honey harvested as a natural sweetener and the beeswax used in candlemaking. Beekeeping was often an integral part of household management. We know that Shakespeare's grandfather Robert Arden kept bees on his farm at Wilmcote. By their nature, bees were symbolic of fertility, prudence, fidelity, success and hard work, and their golden honey associated with wealth and plenty. Bee colonies were also seen as a model for monarchy and civilized society, and in *Henry V*, the Archbishop of Canterbury uses the image of bees to illustrate social order and obedience:

Henry V
1.2

...For so work the honey-bees,
Creatures that by a rule in nature teach
The act of order to a peopled kingdom.
They have a king, and officers of sorts,
Where some like magistrates correct at home;
Others like merchants venture trade abroad;
Others like soldiers armèd in their stings,
Make boot upon the summer's velvet buds...

BREWING

The Two
Gentlemen
of Verona
3.1

...she brews good ale.

❡ IN SHAKESPEARE'S TIME, ale, brewed from ground malt mixed with hot water, was consumed by everybody, as cold water on its own was unsafe to drink. Many households brewed their own ale, and records of Stratford's malt holdings suggest that Shakespeare's wife, Anne, was responsible for brewing ale at New Place, the Shakespeare family home. Hops were added to the ale mix to make beer. The result was a stronger-tasting brew but one that could be kept much longer. The same malt and hops were used a second and third time, the latter producing a weaker brew that was known as small ale or small beer, and often given to children. In *Henry VI part 2*, the rebel Jack Cade proclaims that when he is king, 'the three-hooped pot shall have ten hoops, and I will make it felony to drink small beer.' A three-hooped pot was a tankard for sharing, marked with hoops to ensure that each drinker received his or her equal share.

Small beer came to denote something of little consequence. Thus in Act II of *Othello*, when Iago declares that a deserving woman is fit to 'chronicle small beer', it is intended to belittle her, suggesting she is capable only of noting down trivial things. Yet alehouses were often run by the woman of the household, who opened her premises to the public to sell her surplus ale – and therefore needed to keep a record of the household accounts. Hence the drunkard Christopher Sly's protestation in *The Taming of the Shrew*:

The Taming
of the
Shrew
Induction 2

*Ask Marian Hacket, the fat alewife of
Wincot, if she know me not. If she say
I am not fourteen pence on the score for
sheer ale, score me up for the lying'st
knave in Christendom.*

CANDLE

☞ MADE FROM TALLOW, or beeswax if you could afford it, candles were used all the time in the Tudor home, the only source of light once darkness fell. The most basic, a rush candle, was simply made from rushes dipped into animal fat: it produced little light and a strong, unpleasant odour. In contrast, beeswax candles were much cleaner and brighter. Most rural households of the period would have been almost entirely self-sufficient. Among a housewife's many tasks, including baking, brewing, pickling, preserving, cleaning, washing and sewing, she would also have made the family's candles and soap. In *Macbeth*, as Banquo meets Macbeth in a dark castle, he alludes to this aspect of housekeeping, noting that 'there's husbandry in heaven': thrift and economy mean few stars are shining in the night sky, the 'candles are all out'.

A candle is a practical, everyday item in the plays – 'That light we see is burning in my hall. / How far that little candle throws his beams,' says Portia in *The Merchant of Venice* – but candles are also spiritual and symbolic. In *King Lear*, the Fool claims that the kingdom is in darkness since Lear was banished by his daughters: 'so out went the candle, and we were left darkling.' In one of Shakespeare's most famous soliloquies, Macbeth, too, compares life to a candle flame. Weary of life and time, he laments 'all our yesterdays have lighted fools / The way to dusty death,' and wishes his own life were extinguished as easily: 'Out, out, brief candle.' Macbeth and his wife's dark deeds having caught up with them, the troubled Lady Macbeth sleepwalks through the castle at night. As she appears with her candle, her gentlewoman poignantly tells the watching Doctor, 'She has light by her continually. 'Tis her command.'

against their maker, let them think to lose their honour and dignity in th
return to baseness and inglorious contempt; out of which they were first taken
outward shape and condition please them, yet at the best are but beasts that
suffer hunger.

Cats
but for
like to
cometh
of her
like un
except
flesh is
eyes gl
peciall
to see
and in
hardly
flaming
Democr.
fian. Sm
not tra
the eye
ness, su
Panthe
caſt for
dow ar
ſhine th
ness,
der Aph
ſon, b
Cats ar
by natu
of ſeein
Albe
eye-fig
dark p
night t
to kill
root
(comm
very lik
and wh
if Cats
inſtantl
love th
ſeen in
and no
even t

caused it to be hedged or compassed round about with thornes, for it sme
to a Cat.

The *Egyptians* have observed in the eyes of a Cat, the encrease of the

CAT

❡ ALOOF, mysterious and long associated with superstitious practices, the cat had a strained relationship with the people of Tudor England. Cats were blamed for the plague, and widely believed to be witches' animal guides; it was also said that their breath could cause consumption – that swallowing their hair could suffocate you. In his book of 1607 *The History of Four-Footed Beasts, Serpents and Insects*, Edward Topsell, an English cleric and author, warned that 'the familiars of Witches do most ordinarily appear in the shape of Cats, which is an argument that this beast is dangerous to soul and body.' In the home, however, the cat had status as a valuable mouse-catcher, its stealth and patience referenced by Shakespeare in *Henry IV part 1*: 'I am as vigilant as a cat to steal cream.' In *Romeo and Juliet*, Tybalt is described as the 'Prince of Cats', a feline agility and predatory behaviour evident in his skill with a fencing sword. Later, as they square up to fight, Mercutio calls Tybalt a 'ratcatcher'. 'What wouldst thou have with me,' responds Tybalt; 'Good King of Cats, nothing but one of your nine lives,' Mercutio replies.

Some paintings of the period suggest that cats could be well-loved companions and part of family life. Henry Wriothesley, third Earl of Southampton, imprisoned in the Tower of London for supporting a rebellion against Elizabeth I, is said to have been kept company and even brought food down the chimney by his black-and-white cat, Trixie.

CHERUBIN

¶ SHAKESPEARE refers to cherubin and angels throughout his plays. These otherworldly beings, described in biblical tradition as attendants to God and the guardians of paradise, are beautiful, protective and awe-inspiring figures. On horseback, a 'gallantly armed' and impressive Harry, Prince of Wales, is compared in *Henry IV part 1* with an angel 'dropped down from the clouds to turn and wind a fiery Pegasus'. Romeo describes Juliet as a 'bright angel', as beautiful and as glorious to the night sky as those winged messengers and the 'upturned wond'ring eyes' that gaze on them. As God's representatives on earth, angels were said to herald divine news with horns, and were also closely associated with singing and music, frequently depicted playing musical instruments. As Hamlet dies, Horatio poignantly says goodbye to his friend:

Hamlet
5.2

> *Good night, sweet prince,*
> *And flights of angels*
> *sing thee to thy rest.*

27

DOUBLET

☞ A MAN'S shaped and padded jacket, the doublet was first worn in Spain and gradually appeared across the rest of Europe during the late Middle Ages. Hip length or waist length, in the Tudor period the doublet was close-fitting with baggy sleeves sewn or laced into place. If you were wealthy, your doublet also featured elaborate surface decoration. Embroidery, braid and patterns of small cuts or slashes in the fabric were all popular, as can be seen in portraits and illustrations from the period. Doublets could also be stuffed with wool, sawdust or horsehair, and soft cotton fibres called bombast, to create different silhouettes. A heavily padded stomach, a popular look of the period, was sometimes described as a peascod belly, in reference to the plump, round shapes in a peapod.

In *As You Like It*, Rosalind fears that to cry will 'disgrace my man's apparel', and give away her disguise as a boy. A doublet, she reasons, should show 'itself courageous'. In *Henry IV part 1*, Sir John Falstaff's doublet has borne the brunt of his recent fighting. Recounting his tale to a disbelieving Prince Harry, he describes how he escaped by a miracle, having been 'eight times thrust through the doublet'.

off

DRAGON

Did ever dragon keep so fair a cave?

Romeo and Juliet 3.2

❡ THE DRAGON was a mythical winged serpent 'feared and talked of more than seen'. The Tudors, however, would have been familiar with the image of a dragon. The legend of St George and the Dragon was well known. It was part of the medieval mural in Stratford-upon-Avon's Guild Chapel, and in *King John*, Philip the Bastard recalls the story depicted on the sign of his lodgings: 'Saint George that swinged the dragon, and e'er since / Sits on's horseback at mine hostess' door.' In *Antony and Cleopatra*, Antony ominously observes that 'Sometime we see a cloud that's dragonish,' and in *Henry VI part 1*, the Duke of Gloucester remembers the late King Henry V – 'His arms spread wider than a dragon's wings, / His sparking eyes replete with wrathful fire.' In *Richard III*, the eponymous hero invokes St George to 'Inspire us with the spleen of fiery dragons!'

Dragons were also believed to have magical properties. 'Scale of dragon' is one ingredient in the witches' cauldron in *Macbeth*. In ancient mythology, dragons were said to pull the chariot of night, and in Shakespeare, they are often associated with nighttime. At the end of *Troilus and Cressida*, Achilles says 'The dragon wing of night o'erspreads the earth,' and in *A Midsummer Night's Dream*, Puck must make haste 'For night's swift dragons cut the clouds full fast.'

DROWNING

❡ DROWNING WAS ONE of the most common causes of accidental death in Tudor times and, as Gonzalo reflects in *The Tempest*, an everyday woe for sailors' wives. In *Richard III*, the Duke of Clarence – who is ultimately drowned in a butt of wine – dreams he falls overboard during a sea crossing to France:

Richard III
1.4

Into the tumbling billows of the main.
O Lord! Methought what pain it was to drown!
What dreadful noise of waters in mine ears,
What sights of ugly death within mine eyes.
Methoughts I saw a thousand fearful wrecks,
Ten thousand men that fishes gnawed upon...

Many of Shakespeare's seafaring characters are lucky to escape a similar fate. In *Twelfth Night*, Viola and her brother Sebastian each fear the other has perished in a shipwreck, and in *The Tempest* Ferdinand believes his father has drowned, and mourns 'the wreck of all my friends'.

The risk of drowning was also much closer to home. Men might drown crossing the river to work and, as all the water for the household had to be fetched from the nearest river, women were

also in danger of falling in. This was the fate of a young woman, Katherine Hamlett, who drowned in the Avon juſt a mile out of Stratford-upon-Avon on 17 December 1579. The records of the inqueſt tell how Katherine, going with a pail to draw water at the river 'ſtanding on the bank…suddenly and by accident slipped and fell into the river aforesaid, and…was drowned'. Anyone falling in the water would have her or his misfortune compounded as woollen clothes became increasingly heavy and waterlogged. Gertrude details this very effeĉt in her account of Ophelia's death in *Hamlet*:

<table>
<tr><td>Hamlet
4.7</td><td>

But long it could not be
Till that her garments, heavy with their drink,
Pulled the poor wretch from her melodious lay
To muddy death.
</td></tr>
</table>

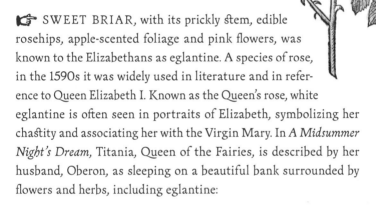

EGLANTINE

☞ SWEET BRIAR, with its prickly stem, edible rosehips, apple-scented foliage and pink flowers, was known to the Elizabethans as eglantine. A species of rose, in the 1590s it was widely used in literature and in reference to Queen Elizabeth I. Known as the Queen's rose, white eglantine is often seen in portraits of Elizabeth, symbolizing her chastity and associating her with the Virgin Mary. In *A Midsummer Night's Dream*, Titania, Queen of the Fairies, is described by her husband, Oberon, as sleeping on a beautiful bank surrounded by flowers and herbs, including eglantine:

> *I know a bank where the wild thyme blows,*
> *Where oxlips and the nodding violet grows,*
> *Quite overcanopied with luscious woodbine,*
> *With sweet musk-roses and with*
> *eglantine.*

A Midsummer
Night's
Dream
2.1

Both musk-roses and eglantine were known for their strong, appealing scents. Titania later adorns the transfigured Bottom, declaring she'll 'stick musk-roses in thy sleek smooth head, / And kiss thy fair large ears, my gentle joy;' and the whole description is beautifully evocative for the senses. The breeze that blows the wild thyme, also aromatic, makes the violets nod their heads too; the woodbine (honeysuckle) is full and fragrant. In *Cymbeline*, believing the disguised Imogen dead, Arviragus promises to 'sweeten thy sad grave'. Along with primroses and harebells, he offers 'the leaf of eglantine, whom not to slander / Outsweetened not thy breath.'

EGÝPT

❡ EGYPT IS A COUNTRY to the south of the Mediterranean Sea, and one of the settings for Shakespeare's tragedy *Antony and Cleopatra*. His story of the Egyptian queen draws on the Roman writer Plutarch's *Lives of the Noble Grecians and Romans*, translated into English by Thomas North in 1597. Seen through Roman eyes, Shakespeare's Egypt is an exotic, sensual, feminine world, personified by its queen, a 'royal wench' of 'infinite variety'.

The Ægyptian Pyramids & colossus

The historical Queen of Egypt, Cleopatra, ruled Egypt from 51 BC to 30 BC, during which time the Egyptian port of Alexandria – notorious in the play for its 'revels' – was a vital centre for commerce and one of the most important cities in the Mediterranean. Egypt was known as the granary of the world, its fertile soil fed by the River Nile, as Antony explains on his return to Rome:

Antony and
Cleopatra
2.7

> *...they take the flow o'th' Nile*
> *By certain scales i'th' pyramid. They know*
> *By th' height, the lowness, or the mean, if dearth*
> *Or foison follow. The higher Nilus swells*
> *The more it promises; as it ebbs, the seedsman*
> *Upon the slime and ooze scatters his grain,*
> *And shortly comes to harvest.*

The Roman senator, Lepidus, is curious to learn more of the country. He remarks 'I have heard the Ptolemies' pyramises are very goodly things,' and asks Antony about the 'strange serpents there', enquiring 'What manner o' thing is your crocodile?'

Egypt held a similar intrigue for the seventeenth-century traveller, too. George Sandys visited in 1611 and records in his *Travailes* (1652) his journey from the 'former flourishing' Alexandria to the Great Pyramids, which he describes as 'the chief of the world's seven wonders'. His journey takes him along the Nile, where he discovers they still measure the height of the river in the way that Antony describes and where he encounters 'divers strange and monstrous creatures' – the hippopotamus – and the 'more than wonderful' crocodile.

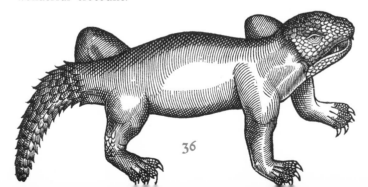

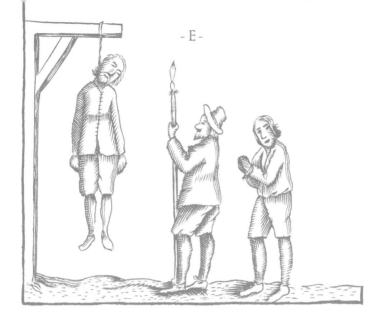

ΕΧΕCUTIOΝ

As wretches have o'ernight,
That wait for execution in the morn.

The Two
Gentlemen
of Verona
4.2

❡ THE PENALTIES for crime in the Tudor period were harsh and cruel, and there was a vaſt array of methods for inflicting punishment. Ranging from being whipped, having your hand cut off, and being put in the ſtocks, through to being boiled or burnt alive and being hanged, drawn and quartered, the punishments were dependent on the severity of the crime and designed to serve as a warning to others. Public executions were commonplace and well attended, the heads of those who loſt them displayed on pikes along London Bridge. The Tower of London was used regularly to imprison enemies of the ſtate, the prisoner arriving at Traitor's Gate (named as such in 1544) by boat along the Thames. The penalty for treason was death by hanging, but only after the victim had been tortured to discover the extent of the plot againſt the monarch. In *Henry VI part 2*, Eleanor, Duchess of Glouceſter, encourages her husband, Humphrey of Gloucester, to take the throne from Henry, and resorts to witchcraft and sorcery to fulfil her political ambitions. Arrested along with her co-conspirators, Eleanor is banished, the others sentenced to death:

Henry VI
part 2
2.3

In sight of God and us your guilt is great;
Receive the sentence of the law for sins
Such as by God's book are adjudged to death.
You four, from hence to prison and back again;
From thence, unto the place of execution.
The witch in Smithfield shall be burned to ashes,
And you three shall be strangled on the gallows.

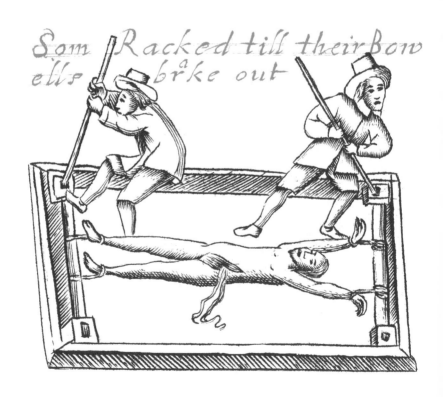

38

EYES, AND EYESIGHT.

Chap. 378.

First it is to be confidered what things are good for the Eyes, and what are not : for the Eyes are the moft neceffary members of all other appertaining to Mans body, and without the fight of them, we can

EYE

¶ IN *A Rich Storehouse or Treasurie for the Diseased* (1612), the authors offer advice on how to take care of the eyes. Eyes, they write, 'who are the only windowes of the minde, both for joy and dread, and the moft of our affections are openly knowne and seene through them, and they are ordained and made of purpose to lighten all the body'. Too much watching, too much weeping, duft, fire, bright light and drunkenness are among the things 'very hurtfull for the Sight'; sleep, red roses, rue, fennel and to 'looke upon any greene or pleasant colours' are all very beneficial. Eyesight was regarded as one of the moft important senses, the eyes associated with wisdom and perception.

Shakespeare often uses eye imagery in his plays, moft notably in *King Lear*, where what the characters see, and fail to see, is powerfully explored. Having ordered his youngest daughter out of his sight, the furious Lear is begged by the Earl of Kent to 'See better, Lear.' In his blind rages, Lear fails to perceive the motives of his elder daughters and does not recognize Cordelia's worth until it is too late. In a particularly gruesome scene, the Earl of Gloucester is literally blinded by the scheming Duke of Cornwall as grotesque punishment for Gloucester's loyalty to Lear. Because he vowed to see 'winged vengeance' bring down Lear's cruel daughters and their husbands, Gloucester's eyes are pulled out:

> Lest it see more, prevent it. Out, vile jelly!
> Where is thy lustre now?

King Lear
3.7

Shakespeare also explored the power of the imagination, the tricks it could play with visions and the inner turmoil it could create. In *Macbeth,* the central character famously speculates:

> Is this a dagger which I see before me,
> The handle toward my hand? Come, let me clutch thee.
> I have thee not, and yet I see thee still.

Macbeth
2.1

And in *Hamlet,* Gertrude prefers not to look inwards and examine her conscience. Having been urged by her son to 'Look here upon this picture, and on this,' the Queen begs:

> O Hamlet, speak no more!
> Thou turn'st mine eyes into my very soul,
> And there I see such black and grainèd spots
> As will not leave their tinct.

Hamlet
3.4

FAVLCON
1. booke.

GER FAVLCON
1. booke.

GOSHAWKE.

LATHAMS
new and second

Booke of Falconrie, concerning the training vp of all HAWKES *that were* vnmentioned in his first Booke of the HAGGART FAVLCON and GERFAVLCON, *formerly* printed; teaching approued Medicines for all their diseases.

By SYMON LATHAM, *Gent·*

AT LONDON,
Printed by *I. B.* for *Roger Iackson*, and are to be sold at his shop neere Fleet-Conduit. 1618,

LANNER.

SPAROWHAWKE

HOBBY.

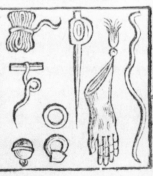

MERLIN.

FALCONRY

Talking of hawking,
nothing else, my lord.

Henry VI
part 2
2.1

☞ THE ART OF REARING and train-
ing birds of prey to hunt quarry, falconry
was a popular – and expensive – pastime among the Elizabethan
nobility. The falconer's methods of bringing a bird under his control
included covering the bird's head – or hoodwinking it – to prevent
it seeing, or even sewing silk threads into the bird's lower eyelids
so that they might be pulled shut. Macbeth alludes to this practice,
known as scarfing, when he says 'Come seeling night / Scarf up
the tender eye of pitiful day.' Birds were held in the falconer's hand
by jesses, which were short leather straps fixed to the birds' legs,
often with bells attached, and were encouraged to return to their
handler by means of a lure of food. Hence Juliet calls after Romeo:
'Hist, Romeo! Hist! O for a falconer's voice / To lure this tassel-
gentle back again!' Tassel-gentle – or tercel – was another name for
a peregrine falcon.

In more sinister vein, Othello also
alludes to this manner of controlling
a falcon, when, as he begins to be
consumed by jealousy, he says about
Desdemona to Iago:

If I do prove her haggard,
Though that her jesses were
my dear heart-strings
I'd whistle her off and let
her down the wind
To prey at fortune.

Othello
3.3

A haggard was a wild hawk that was at least a year old, used to hunting its own prey and therefore harder to train. The same imagery occurs in a much earlier play, *The Taming of the Shrew*, where Christopher Sly is asked in the Induction, 'Dost thou like hawking?' and in the play itself, Petruccio adopts the falconer's methods as a way of taming the spirited 'haggard' Kate, by depriving her of food:

The Taming
of the
Shrew
4.1

> *My falcon now is sharp and passing empty,*
> *And till she stoop she must not be full-gorged,*
> *For then she never looks upon her lure.*
> *Another way I have to man my haggard,*
> *To make her come and know her keeper's call —*
> *That is, to watch her as we watch these kites*
> *That bate and beat, and will not be obedient.*
> *She ate no meat today, nor none shall eat.*
> *Last night she slept not, nor tonight she shall not.*

The forme and fashion of the Haggard-Faulcon.

FASHION

*How oddly he is suited!
I think he bought his doublet
in Italy, his round hose in
France, his bonnet in Germany,
and his behaviour everywhere.*

The
Merchant
of Venice
1.2

¶ UNDER BOTH Henry VIII and Elizabeth I, sumptuary laws dictated what types of garment, the fabric, the colours, the trims, could be worn by each level of society. The laws aimed to discourage unnecessary spending and to ensure that nobody dressed above his or her station. In a proclamation issued in 1574, the Queen referred to the young gentlemen who run themselves into debt buying superfluous gold cloth and silks as 'allured by the vain show of those things'. In *Hamlet*, as Polonius's son Laertes departs for Europe, his father advises him:

*Costly thy habit as thy purse can buy,
But not expressed in fancy; rich not gaudy;
For the apparel oft proclaims the man...*

Hamlet
1.3

Cloth of gold, fur, silk, velvet and purple- or crimson-dyed fabrics were reserved for those of the highest status. As a young princess, Elizabeth often wore red and as Queen opted to dress her ladies-in-waiting in scarlet, while she went on to wear gowns in gold and silver. In *Much Ado About Nothing*, Margaret describes to Hero the Duchess of Milan's dress: 'cloth o' gold, and cuts, and

The Bowll bay
ryng.

The Beare
bayting.

Wynchester P.

laced with silver, set with pearls, down sleeves, side sleeves, and
skirts round underborne with a bluish tinsel'. Hero's own gown,
she reassures her, is less elaborate but just as fine.

Plant and vegetable dyes were used to achieve colour. Ordinary
Elizabethans dyed their wools and linens with woad to create
blue, and with walnut to create browns and beige, the mordants
(substances) used to fix the dyes allowing green and yellow to be
achieved too. Dark and rich colours were more expensive to create
because of the length of the process. Gallons of water, repeated
immersions and noxious fumes were all part of creating a deep
indigo, the dyer's senses and hands overwhelmed with the colour:

Sonnet 111

And almost thence my nature is subdued
To what it works in, like the dyer's hand.

48

FOLIO

Devise wit, write pen, for I am for whole volumes, in folio.

Love's Labour's Lost 1.2

❡ A FOLIO is a large book made up of sheets of paper folded in half to create two leaves or four pages of printed text. The folio's format was reserved for prestigious works of religion, history or philosophy. The more common, cheaper format was the quarto, in which the sheets of paper were folded in half again to produce four leaves and eight pages of print from the same-size sheet.

Some of Shakespeare's plays had been printed individually as quartos before his death. But it was not until 1616 and the publication of Ben Jonson's grandly titled *Workes* that a dramatist's collected plays were printed in folio. In 1623, seven years after Shakespeare's death, thirty-six of his plays were published together in a folio edition as *Mr William Shakespeare's Comedies, Histories and Tragedies*. The plays were compiled and edited by Shakespeare's friends and fellow actors, John Heminges and Henry Condell, and 'Published according to the True Originall Copies'. The project was underwritten by a syndicate of publishers in order to share the financial burden and secure rights to the individual plays, and took almost two years to complete. Originally advertised for publication in 1622, the title was finally recorded in the Stationers' Register on 8 November 1623. It is believed about 750 copies were printed, with bound copies being sold for £1 each. The book was a great success, selling out within a decade, and three further revised editions were published in the seventeenth century. It is the first edition, the First Folio, however, which gave us eighteen of Shakespeare's plays for the first time in print, as well as an iconic image of their author, and is rightfully celebrated as one of the most important books in the history of literature.

A CATALOGVE

of the seuerall Comedies, Histories, and Tragedies contained in this Volume.

COMEDIES.

He Tempest.   *Folio* 1.

The two Gentlemen of Verona.   20

The Merry Wiues of Windsor.   38

Measure for Measure.   61

The Comedy of Errours.   85

Much adoo about Nothing.   101

Loues Labour lost.   122

Midsommer Nights Dreame.   145

The Merchant of Venice.   163

As you Like it.   185

The Taming of the Shrew.   208

All is well, that Ends well.   230

Twelfe-Night, or what you will.   255

The Winters Tale.   304

HISTORIES.

The Life and Death of King Iohn.   *Fol.* 1.

The Life & death of Richard the second.   23

The First part of King Henry the fourth.   46

The Second part of K. Henry the fourth.   74

The Life of King Henry the Fift.   69

The First part of King Henry the Sixt.   96

The Second part of King Hen. the Sixt.   120

The Third part of King Henry the Sixt.   147

The Life & Death of Richard the Third. 173

The Life of King Henry the Eight.   205

TRAGEDIES.

The Tragedy of Coriolanus.   *Fol.* 1.

Titus Andronicus.   31

Romeo and Iuliet.   53

Timon of Athens.   80

The Life and death of Iulius Cæsar.   109

The Tragedy of Macbeth.   131

The Tragedy of Hamlet.   152

King Lear.   283

Othello, the Moore of Venice.   310

Anthony and Cleopater.   346

Cymbeline King of Britaine.   369

FROST

❡ WINTER was bitterly cold
in Tudor England. Along with most
of Europe at this time, the country
was living through a period now
known as the little ice age, owing
to the length and severity of the
winters. In London the River Thames
froze over several times, and in 1536
Henry VIII is said to have travelled by sleigh
along the icebound river to his palace at Greenwich.
Wider, and slower moving than it is today, the Thames froze
easily and thickly, with great blocks of ice settling in underneath the
piers of London Bridge. In the winter of 1607–8 the first recorded frost
fair was held on the ice, initiated by the hundreds of bargemen and
sailors who made their living on the river and were now effectively
out of work. Tents and camp fires appeared, shops and ale-houses
were hastily constructed, and people could play football, or ice skate,
or bowl, enjoy roasted meat, and buy fruits and spicy gingerbread.

Hard winters had an effect on all aspects of life whether in
town or country. In the entertainment at the end of *Love's Labour's
Lost*, the character Hiems, or Winter, sings of the season's impact
on rural life:

> When icicles hang by the wall,
> And Dick the shepherd blows his nail,
> And Tom bears logs into the hall,
> And milk comes frozen home in pail;
> When blood is nipped, and ways be foul,
> Then nightly sings the staring owl:
> Tu-whit, tu-whoo! — a merry note,
> While greasy Joan doth keel the pot.

Love's
Labour's
Lost
5.2

GARDENER

☞ FOR MANY HOUSEHOLDS in the sixteenth century, the garden was a vital source of fruit, vegetables and medicinal herbs. Housewives grew plants for dyeing and strewing, and flowers were cultivated for their scent and decoration. The gardens of larger houses were places to entertain and impress, with alleys and arbours, stately hedges and fountains, and intricately patterned knot gardens.

The publication of myriad herbals and gardening manuals reflected the new horticultural techniques and the huge variety of new plants introduced to England from Europe and around the world as trade and travel routes expanded in Shakespeare's lifetime. Well-read gentlemen became gardeners too, and in the plays Shakespeare demonstrates an extensive knowledge of plants, flowers and practical husbandry. In *Henry V*, the Constable cautions the Dauphin that the King covers his discretion behind a coat of folly, 'As gardeners do with ordure [manure] hide those roots / That shall first spring and be most delicate,' and in *Richard II* the gardener tells his servant:

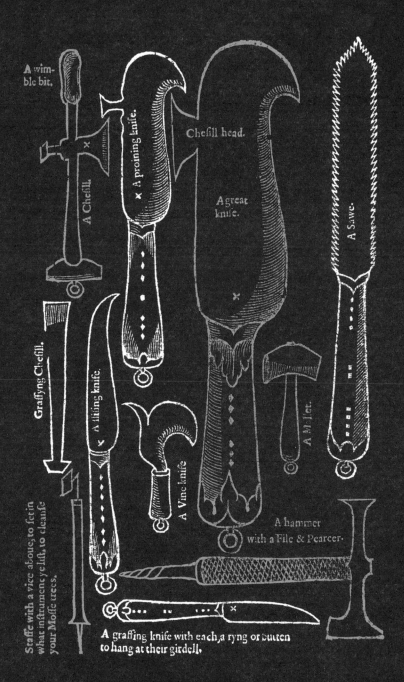

A wim-ble bit.

A Chefill.

A proining knife.

Chefill head.

A great knife.

A Sawe.

Graffing Chefill.

A fliting knife.

A Vine knife.

A Mi let.

A hammer with a File & Pearcer.

Staffe with a vice aboue, to fet in what inftrumency lift, to cleanfe your Moffe trees.

A graffing knife with each, a ryng or butten to hang at their girdell.

Richard II
3.4

> *Go, bind thou up young dangling apricots*
> *Which, like unruly children, make their sire*
> *Stoop with oppression of their prodigal weight.*
> *Give some supportance to the bending twigs.*

For Shakespeare, the well-tended garden is a recurring symbol of a well-ordered kingdom. In the same scene, the servant laments the king's neglect of 'our sea-wallèd garden, the whole land' that is now 'full of weeds, her fairest flowers choked up'. Although critical of the king, the gardener's reply exemplifies good husbandry:

Richard II
3.4

> *O, what pity is it*
> *That he had not so trimmed and dressed his land*
> *As we this garden! We at time of year*
> *Do wound the bark, the skin of our fruit trees,*
> *Lest, being over-proud in sap and blood,*
> *With too much riches it confound itself.*
> *Had he done so to great and growing men,*
> *They might have lived to bear, and he to taste,*
> *Their fruits of duty. Superfluous branches*
> *We lop away, that bearing boughs may live.*
> *Had he done so, himself had borne the crown,*
> *Which waste of idle hours hath quite thrown down.*

G͜LOBE

*Can this cock-pit hold
The vasty fields of France? Or may we cram
Within this wooden O the very casques
That did affright the air at Agincourt?*

❡ THE GLOBE was the playhouse of Shakespeare's acting company, built in 1599 and financed by a syndicate of partners that included Shakespeare and Richard Burbage. It was constructed from oak timbers, south of the River Thames in Bankside, a leisure district known for its brothels and bear-baiting. The newly constructed Globe was not quite the 'wooden O' referred to by the Chorus in *Henry V* but a twenty-sided open-air amphitheatre, measuring 30 metres across. A surviving contemporary sketch of another Bankside playhouse, the Swan, suggests a thrust stage projected into the yard, with a canopy above it supported by pillars, the underside of which was painted with stars to resemble the 'heavens'. The space beneath the stage was the corresponding 'hell' from which ghosts and haunting music would have emerged. At the back of the

- G -

stage a balcony housed the musicians and was used to represent battlements or an upper window.

With minimal scenery on stage, the Globe's audience was asked to use its imagination, just as the prologue to *Henry V* entreats playgoers to 'Think, when we talk of horses, that you see them, / Printing their proud hoofs i'th' receiving earth.' That same prologue ends with the plea, 'Gently to hear, kindly to judge, our play.' The audience at the Globe numbered as many as three thousand, made up of people from all classes of society, and the playgoers who paid a penny to stand in the yard were often a rowdy, irreverent crowd. Hamlet describes them disparagingly as 'the groundlings, who for the most part are capable of nothing but inexplicable dumb shows and noise'. For an extra penny, playgoers could sit in the three-tiered gallery and, for an additional payment, in the gentlemen's rooms to the side of the stage, where the wealthy nobility sat in full view of the crowd. In all, London theatregoers would have witnessed the first-ever performance of fifteen of Shakespeare's plays, including his greatest tragedies, on the Globe stage.

On 29 June 1613, during a performance of *Henry VIII* or *All Is True*, a cannon fired to herald the entrance of the King caused the thatched roof of the theatre to ignite. A detailed account of the event given by Sir Henry Wotton in a letter a few days later suggests spectators were initially unconcerned, it 'being thought at first but an idle smoke, and their eyes more attentive on the show'. The fire quickly took hold, however, and within two hours the Globe was burnt to the ground. Audience and actors seem to have escaped unscathed, Wotton noting that 'only one man had his breeches set on fire, that would perhaps have broiled him if he had not by the benefit of a provident wit put it out with bottle ale'.

The Globe was rebuilt the following year at considerable cost to the company – and with a tiled roof this time. When it reopened, however, Shakespeare was no longer a shareholder, signalling the end of his London theatre career.

GLOVES

❡ A FASHIONABLE accessory in Shakespeare's time, gloves were worn by both men and women. Especially popular among the rich, gloves were made from the finest skins and beautifully embroidered and decorated, designed to show the wealth and social status of the wearer. On a practical level, gloves protected the hands – a falconer wore a large leather gauntlet, a knight one made of metal – but they were also symbolic, thrown down as mark of a challenge to a foe or presented as gifts during courtship. Queen Elizabeth I is said to have had a vast collection of gloves and to have given away many as scented favours or tokens of her esteem.

In *Much Ado about Nothing*, Hero shows her friends her fiancé's gift: 'These gloves the Count sent me, they are an excellent perfume,' and in *Romeo and Juliet* the romantic associations are heightened as Romeo watches Juliet on her balcony from the shadows:

> *See how she leans her cheek upon her hand.*
> *O, that I were a glove upon that hand,*
> *That I might touch that cheek!*

Romeo
and Juliet
2.1

Shakespeare's father, John, was a glover and leatherworker, or whittawer, his workshop based in the family home on Henley Street. It has been suggested that Shakespeare may have worked alongside his father, as there are references to the craft and its materials throughout the plays. In *The Merry Wives of Windsor*, Mistress Quickly enquires about Master Slender, and asks: 'Does he not wear a great round beard, like a glover's paring-knife?' As Romeo laughs with his friends, Mercutio tells him that his jokes are thin, comparing Romeo's wit to a 'cheverel that stretches from an inch narrow to an ell broad'. Cheveril, soft leather made of kid skin, was known for its pliancy.

HANDS

☞ HAND GESTURES and hand imagery feature extensively in the plays, signifying love and unity but also violent death. In *Macbeth,* for example, hands are a recurring motif. Having murdered Duncan, Macbeth and Lady Macbeth contemplate their bloodstained hands. 'This is a sorry sight,' says Macbeth, before asking 'Will all great Neptune's ocean wash this blood / Clean from my hand?' Lady Macbeth's response is 'A little water clears us of this deed,' but later in the play Macbeth is said to feel 'His secret murders sticking on his hands,' and Lady Macbeth's guilt is evident in her obsessive hand-rubbing, culminating in her declaration: 'Out, damned spot; out, I say.'

The prologue to *Romeo and Juliet* uses similar imagery to evoke the family feud in Verona, 'Where civil blood makes civil hands unclean.' In love with Romeo, a conflicted Juliet asks 'What's Montague? It is nor hand, nor foot' but she is subsequently horrified to discover the truth of her cousin's murder – 'O God, did Romeo's hand shed Tybalt's blood?' – and Romeo admits 'that name's cursèd hand / Murdered her kinsman.' With the two families in mourning at the end of the play, Capulet offers his hand in a gesture of reconciliation: 'Oh brother Montague, give me thy hand.'

In *Romeo and Juliet,* Shakespeare also conveys the intimacy of touching hands. Seeing Juliet for the first time, Romeo remarks 'I'll watch her place of stand, / And, touching hers, make blessed my rude hand,' and the wordplay of their first encounter evokes the idea of pilgrims – or palmers – laying hands on the statues of saints: 'palm to palm is holy palmers' kiss'. So often in the plays, the joining of hands signifies love and marriage. In *The Tempest* this is tenderly observed in the scene between Miranda and Ferdinand as they agree to marry. 'Here's my hand,' says Ferdinand, 'And mine, with

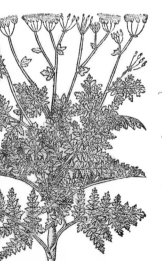

my heart in't,' Miranda responds, in a form of betrothal known as hand-fasting. In Shakespeare's time, hand-fasting was a ceremony in which lovers joined hands and exchanged vows in front of a witness. Although the union was still expected to be solemnized in church (as Prospero is keen to point out to Ferdinand), the act of hand-fasting was often deemed sufficient for the marriage to be valid.

In the epilogue to *A Midsummer Night's Dream*, a play that ends with a wedding in which the 'couples shall eternally be knit', Shakespeare also reminds us of another contract, that between the actor and the audience. Puck appeals to the audience to show their appreciation with their applause: 'Give me your hands, if we be friends, / And Robin shall restore amends.'

HEMLOCK

*Crowned with rank furmitor
 and furrow-weeds,
With burdocks, hemlock,
 nettles, cuckoo-flowers,
Darnel, and all the idle
 weeds that grow
In our sustaining corn.*
King Lear 4.3

❡ GROWING TALL, with white flower-heads and bright, feathery green leaves, hemlock thrives today on waste ground and at road-sides. All parts of the plant are poisonous; the stem dark red and mottled, the scent repellent and lingering: unsurprisingly, the plant has a long association with witchcraft, and features in the list of toxic ingredients added to the cauldron by the witches in *Macbeth*. Animal parts, human organs and herbs all go in, the effects of the hemlock all the more potent because it has been 'digged i'th' dark'. It was believed that poisonous plants harvested in the dark became stronger, an idea also mentioned in *Hamlet* when the Player King portrays a character who is poisoned exactly as Hamlet's father was. In the first act of the play, Old Hamlet describes the horrible death inflicted upon him:

Sleeping within mine orchard,
My custom always in the afternoon,
Upon my secure hour thy uncle stole
With juice of cursèd hebenon in a vial,
And in the porches of mine ears did pour
The leperous distilment...

Hamlet
1.5

In the play within the play, the poison used has been cursed three times and is a 'mixture rank of midnight weeds collected'. The weeds aren't specified but along with hemlock could include yew, deadly nightshade, mandrake and henbane. Writing in *The Herball or Generall historie of plantes* (1597), John Gerard, an English botanist who had a large herbal garden in London, describes the unquiet sleep produced by henbane, and it was historically used, along with mandrake and hemlock, to create an anaesthetic potion. Thus, on the eve of her arranged marriage to Paris, Juliet prepares to take the sleeping-potion that will make her appear dead: 'Take thou this vial,' says Friar Laurence, 'being then in bed, / And this distilling liquor drink thou off, / When presently through all thy veins shall run / A cold and drowsy humour...' Fearfully and poignantly, Juliet worries that the draught will not work or, worse, that it will poison and kill her:

Romeo and
Juliet
4.3

Come, vial. What if this mixture do not work at all?
Shall I be married then tomorrow morning?...
What if it be poison which the friar
Subtly hath ministered to have me dead,
Lest in this marriage he should be dishonoured
Because he married me before to Romeo?

HORSE

A horse! A horse! My kingdom for a horse!

Richard III
5.7

¶ HORSES were revered and valuable animals in the Tudor period and were used in practically all aspects of daily life. With important roles to play in agriculture, travel, sport, pleasure and war, horse ownership was widespread and eventually protected by law as horse theft became increasingly common. Knights and soldiers might ride mounts bred specifically for the role or type of work they would be used for, such as a powerful and strong courser or destrier; a woman might travel on a comfortable palfrey or jennet; and a farmer would employ a heavy and strong draught breed.

Horses are mentioned throughout Shakespeare's works, the most evocative description being the account of Adonis's fine animal in the poem *Venus and Adonis*:

Venus
and Adonis
295-300

> *Round-hoofed, short jointed,*
> *fetlocks shag and long,*
> *Broad breast, full eye,*
> *small head, and nostril wide,*
> *High crest, short ears,*
> *straight legs, and passing strong;*
> *Thin mane, thick tail,*
> *broad buttock, tender hide —*
> *Look what a horse should have he did not lack,*
> *Save a proud rider on so proud a back.*

| 36 | 38 | Septen | 40 | trio. |

Hv

Villach

Trauwenstain

Steir

Traburg

Oberndorf

Maur

Marpurg

ma

47

Windischgretz

Presberg

Petau

Warasin

Wurtzen

Neuburg

Presne

Krain.

Saneck

Win

Saw flu

Cilly

Semnicz

Layhach

Ober Laybach

Sosfed

dischm

Dulmein

Seiffenberg

Zakaoce

Cirknicz

Sambar

Wuczdi lobia

Sagowns Palm

46

Gafers

Rosack

Sicis

S.Veii

Gradisla

Histria.

Terfacz

Gradecz

Pola

Craba:

Nouo gradecz

Waxicz

Terges:

Wihicz

ten.

Iaicz

tinvs

Camnecz

sinvs

Sockol

Zeng

45

Camen grad

Wischgrod

ILLYRICVM

Wosseu.

Occi: dens.

ILLYRIA

Viola: What country, friends, is this?
Captain: This is Illyria, lady.

Twelfth
Night
1.2

☞ THE SETTING for Shakespeare's *Twelfth Night*, Illyria was historically a region along the east coast of the Adriatic Sea. In *His Epitomie of The Theater of the World* (1603), Abraham Ortelius notes of Illyria that 'All the sea coast is hot, as it is in Italy, and fruitful, yielding good corn, fair olive trees and excellent vineyards.' The trading vessels attracted to the region were at risk not only of shipwreck but of piracy too, the Duke of Suffolk alluding to this in *Henry VI part 2* when he likens the Captain who has taken him prisoner to 'Bargulus, the strong Illyrian pirate'.

Illyria has its origins in Classical antiquity and in *Twelfth Night* Sebastian talks of a city of renown, asking 'Shall we go see the relics of this town?' The play, however, offers little further description of its Illyrian setting and what hints there are bear closer resemblance to Shakespeare's London than to a foreign country. Viola's call of 'Westward ho!' echoes the popular cry of the boatmen on the River Thames and when Antonio recommends to Sebastian that 'In the south suburbs at the Elephant / Is best to lodge', Shakespeare probably has in mind the pub of the same name that stood near to the Globe theatre. Just as Viola, dressed as a boy, says to the countess Olivia 'I am not that I play,' the fictional Illyria in *Twelfth Night* appears to be somewhere else too. An indeterminate, imagined place, it is a fitting backdrop to a play about disguise and mistaken identity, in which one character, Fabian, is heard to say: 'If this were played upon a stage now, I could condemn it as an improbable fiction.'

INK

Henry VI
part 1

5.5 *I'll call for pen and ink, and write my mind.*

❡ THE ELIZABETHANS wrote using a quill pen and ink. Many of Shakespeare's characters, Cleopatra, Romeo, Pericles and Malvolio among them, call for 'ink and paper'. The more expensive parchment or vellum was reserved for legal documents. Writing ink was made from a mixture of iron salts (known as green vitriol) and vegetable tannins derived from oak gall, which was then added to a binder, usually gum Arabic. The result was a dark, permanent ink. In Sonnet 65, Shakespeare celebrates the permanence of the written word, declaring that 'in black ink my love may still shine bright.'

But there are dark associations too. Hamlet, in mourning, refers to his 'inky cloak', and there is a sense of bitterness in Sir Toby Belch's pun on gall as one of ink's key ingredients: 'Let there be gall enough in thy ink; though thou write with a goose-pen, no matter.' Ink was stored in an inkwell or in a portable container called an inkhorn. In *Much Ado About Nothing*, Dogberry asks for the 'learned writer' Francis Seacoal to 'bring his pen and inkhorn to the jail'. By association, inkhorn became a familiar term for a scholar, and, more particularly, one who was pedantic or pretentious. Hence one of Gloucester's servants in *Henry VI part 1* defends his master against 'an inkhorn mate'.

The forme of diuers sorts of Gals.

3 *Galla orbiculata.*
The round Gall.

4 *Galla oblonga.*
The long Gall.

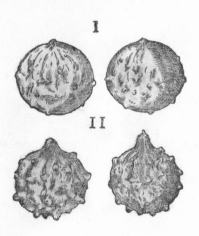

I

II

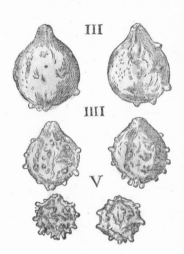

III

IIII

V

5 *Galla viridis, siue omphacitis.*
Greene or vnripe Gals.

6 *Galla Asinina.*
Asses Gals.

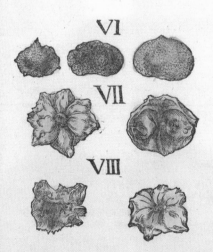

VI

VII

VIII

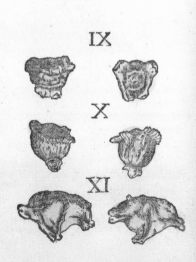

IX

X

XI

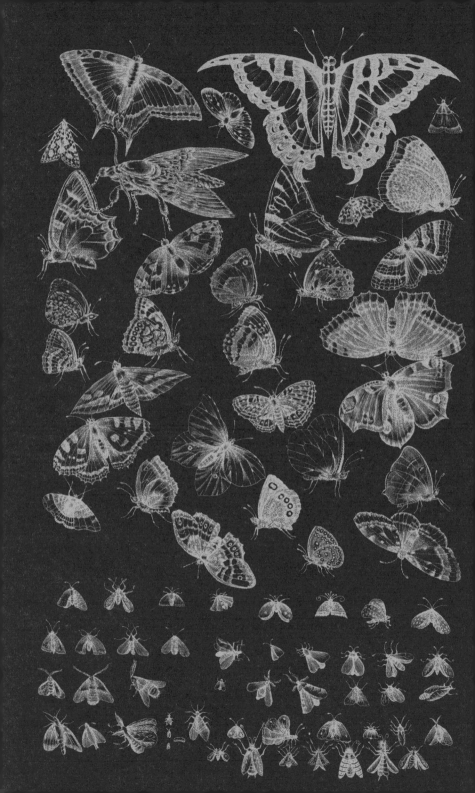

INSECTS

...how the poor world is pestered with such waterflies!
Diminutives of nature.

Troilus
and Cressida
5.1

❡ REFERENCES to insects, snails and spiders run through the plays, from the 'red-tailed humble-bee' in *All's Well That Ends Well* to the 'shard-borne beetle' in *Macbeth*. Insects buzz, sting and pester and are often referred to in the form of insults or expressions of irritation. In *The Taming of the Shrew* Petruccio harangues the tailor – 'Thou flea, thou nit, thou winter-cricket' – and calls his wife Kate a wasp, to which she replies: 'If I be waspish, best beware my sting.' In *Henry IV part 1*, Hotspur is 'stung with pismires' at the mention of Bolingbroke, pismire being a colloquial word for a type of ant, so called after the distinctive smell of its anthill.

Shakespeare's observations of insects and arthropods reveal a poet in tune with the natural world. In *Antony and Cleopatra*, the image Scarus uses to describe Cleopatra's flight from the sea battle is one of livestock startled by a gadfly, 'The breese upon her, like a cow in June,' and in *Venus and Adonis* Shakespeare describes in exquisite detail how Venus recoils from the horrific sight of her dead lover, Adonis:

> *...as the snail, whose tender horns being hit*
> *Shrinks backward in his shelly cave with pain,*
> *And there, all smothered up, in shade doth sit,*
> *Long after fearing to creep forth again...*

Venus
and Adonis
1033-36

Insects are integral to, and take us into, Shakespeare's fairy world too. In *The Merry Wives of Windsor*, as the party sets off for the magical Herne's oak, Evans declares that 'twenty glow-worms shall our lanterns be', and in *A Midsummer Night's Dream* Titania calls for her fairies to 'pluck the wings of painted butterflies' to use as fans. It is in Mercutio's description of the fairy Queen Mab in *Romeo and Juliet*, however, that Shakespeare conjures up a scene of the most fantastically miniscule proportions:

Romeo and
Juliet
1.4

She is the fairies' midwife, and she comes
In shape no bigger than an agate stone
On the forefinger of an alderman,
Drawn with a team of little atomi
Athwart men's noses as they lie asleep.
Her wagon spokes made of long spinners' legs;
The cover, of the wings of grasshoppers;
Her traces, of the moonshine's wat'ry beams;
Her collars, of the smallest spider web;
Her whip, of cricket's bone, the lash of film;
Her wagoner, a small grey-coated gnat
Not half so big as a round little worm
Pricked from the lazy finger of a maid.

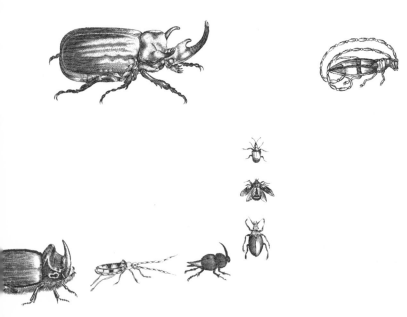

JAMES I

❡ WHEN QUEEN ELIZABETH I died on 24 March 1603, she was succeeded by her distant cousin, James VI of Scotland, the only son of Mary Queen of Scots. He was crowned King James I of England on 25 July 1603. As King of Scotland he had composed a masque and written three books, including *Daemonologie* (1597), a study of witchcraft. On his succession to the English throne, James's interest in the theatre was demonstrated almost immediately, when he became patron of Shakespeare's actors' company, the Lord Chamberlain's Men, known thenceforth as the King's Men. Shakespeare and his fellow actors were promoted to the gentry, and, as new members of the royal household, were each issued with four-and-a-half yards of red cloth for their royal livery.

As well as authorizing the company to perform publicly 'within their nowe usual house called the Globe' and across the country, the royal patent issued on 19 May 1603 licensed the actors: 'Freely to use and exercise the Art and Facultie of playing Comedies, Tragedies, Histories, Enterludes, Morals, Pastoralls, Stage Plaies and such others, like as these have alreadie studied or hereafter shall use or studie, as well for our Solace and Pleasure, when wee shall thincke good to see them, during our Pleasure...'

In practice, that meant performing regularly for the King's entertainment at court during the winter months, and at least thirteen of Shakespeare's plays were performed before the King. *Macbeth* was most likely written to appeal to James's fascination with witchcraft, and his proud Scottish lineage. One of the witches tells Banquo 'Thou shalt get kings, though thou be none,' and later in the play the witches conjure up an apparition of eight Scottish kings descended from Banquo, leading up to the present king, James.

JESTER

Twelfth
Night
2.4 *'Feste the jester, my lord, a fool that the lady Olivia's
father took much delight in. He is about the house.*

☞ IN THE COURTS of medieval and renaissance Europe, the position of jester or fool was a recognized office. Employed to provide humour and entertainment, jesters used physical comedy, song and clever wordplay to amuse and make fun. Licensed to tease and comment openly, jesters had a freedom of speech unmatched by many others within a court or household. Henry VIII's jester Will Sommers was said to have a shrewd wit and to be popular with the King's ministers, who acknowledged the influence of his well-placed 'jokes'. Traditionally, jesters were costumed in bright colours in a patchwork design, and a jester's multicoloured coat was described as motley, hence Jaques's remark in *As You Like It*: 'O that I were a fool, / I am ambitious for a motley coat.'

There are numerous fools, and clowns, in Shakespeare's plays. In the early comedies *A Midsummer Night's Dream* (1595) and *Much Ado About Nothing* (1598–9) the characters of Bottom and Dogberry respectively provide plenty of opportunity for an actor to bumble, bluster and show off. The pompous constable Dogberry muddles his words to comic effect: 'Is our whole dissembly appeared?', and 'O villain! Thou wilt be condemned into everlasting

74

redemption for this.' The exuberant Nick Bottom excitedly prepares to perform before nobility at a wedding, and, transformed by the magic of the fairies, appears later in the play with an ass's head. Hamlet recognizes the scene-stealing potential of a clown and tells the acting company arrived at Elsinore: 'And let those that play your clowns speak no more than is set down for them.'

Shakespeare's fools are also world weary, melancholy and wise. In *Twelfth Night*, Feste neatly suggests to Olivia that she is foolish still to mourn her brother: 'The more fool, madonna, to mourn for your brother's soul, being in heaven,' and reminds her that though he may dress as a fool, 'I wear not motley in my brain.' The Fool in *King Lear* is devoted and loyal, accompanying Lear into the wilderness, watching his descent into madness and wryly reminding the King of his folly in trying to divide the kingdom between his daughters. 'Thou shouldst not have been old till thou hadst been wise,' the Fool observes early in the play, and more pointedly tells Lear he 'can tell why a snail has a house' before delivering the punchline: 'Why, to put 's head in, not to give it away to his daughters and leave his horns without a case.' Nobody else in the play speaks quite so directly to the King; nobody but the court jester would be able to sing:

> *He that has and a little tiny wit,*
> *With heigh-ho, the wind and the rain,*
> *Must make content with his fortunes fit,*
> *Though the rain it raineth every day.*

King Lear
3.2

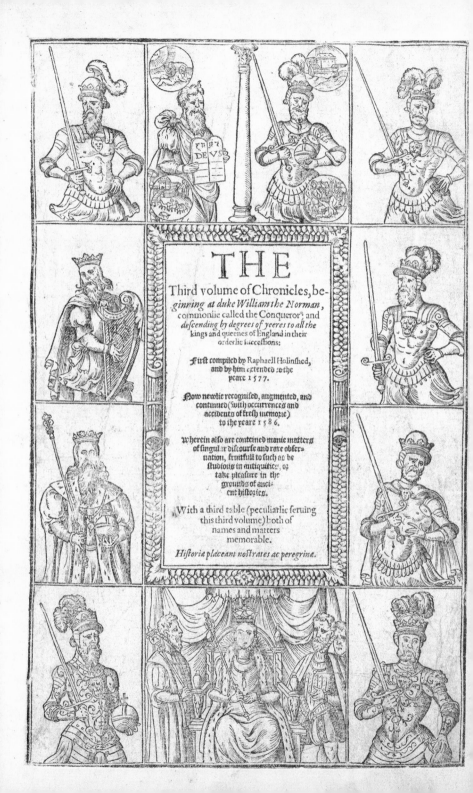

THE

Third volume of Chronicles, be-
ginning at duke *William the Norman*,
commonlie called the Conqueror; and
descending by degrees of yeeres to all the
kings and queenes of England in their
orderlie successions:

First compiled by Raphaell Holinshed,
and by him extended to the
yeare 1577.

Now newlie recognised, augmented, and
continued (with occurrences and
accidents of fresh memorie)
to the yeare 1586.

Wherein also are conteined manie matters
of singular discourse and rare obser-
uation, fruitfull to such as be
studious in antiquities, or
take pleasure in the
grounds of anci-
ent histories.

With a third table (peculiarlie seruing
this third volume) both of
names and matters
memorable.

Historiæ placeant nostrates ac peregrinæ.

KINGS

Tomorrow may it please
you to be crowned?

Richard III
3.7

☞ ALONG WITH the Comedies and
the Tragedies, the *First Folio* includes the
Histories, Shakespeare's ten plays about the Kings of England. The
plays appear in the order of their action, not the order in which they
were composed, and take Holinshed's *Chronicles* (1577), an historical
account of the Kings of England, Scotland and Ireland, as their
principal literary source. Shakespeare blended the historical details
with his own inventions, and in some instances used the accounts
simply as inspiration. Aside from *Henry VIII*, all the history plays
were written during Elizabeth's reign, and some scholars argue
that the dramas have a political bias, demonstrating the dangers
of civil war and depicting Richard III, the last member of the House
of York, as a monstrous villain.

Political machinations, battle scenes and rousing speeches
aside, Shakespeare focused too on the weight of responsibility that
went with wearing the crown. The sleepless Henry IV knows too
well that 'uneasy lies the head that wears a crown;' Henry VI knows
that contentment is a rare gift: 'My crown is called content – /
A crown it is that seldom kings enjoy.' Richard II describes 'the
hollow crown that rounds the mortal temples of a king'. The crown
is worn for just a short time, in ceremony and 'vain conceit': a king
rules as he wishes and believes himself invincible, before death
reminds him he is just a man:

Richard II
3.2

For God's sake, let us sit upon the ground,
And tell sad stories of the death of kings —
How some have been deposed, some slain in war,
Some haunted by the ghosts they have deposed,
Some poisoned by their wives, some sleeping killed,
All murdered. For within the hollow crown
That rounds the mortal temples of a king
Keeps Death his court; and the antic sits,
Scoffing his state and grinning at his pomp,
Allowing him a breath, a little scene,
To monarchize, be feared, and kill with looks,
Infusing him with self and vain conceit,
As if this flesh which walls about our life
Were brass impregnable; and humoured thus,
Comes at the last, and with a little pin
Bores through his castle wall; and farewell, king.

LONDON

*Enquire at London 'mongst
the taverns there*

Richard II
5.3

☞ LONDON was transformed in Shakespeare's time and its population grew rapidly, reflecting a diverse cross-section of society. It quickly became an important centre of culture and trade, with a healthy economy that attracted merchants from northern Europe and beyond. The only bridge across the river in the city at this time, London Bridge was thronged with street vendors, shops and houses, and punctuated by long wooden pikes that displayed the heads of traitors.

Shakespeare is believed to have arrived in London in the early 1590s and he quickly established himself as an upcoming writer and actor. He lived and worked in the north of the city but would have regularly crossed the river to Southwark and the theatres. He rented properties in Blackfriars, and also lodged in Silver Street in 1604, in the house of French Huguenot Christopher Mountjoy. Playgoing was very much a part of everyday life in the capital and the theatres flourished during this period. The appetite for longer, more ambitious and complex plays was growing and Shakespeare was perfectly placed to take advantage. The London that he knew is recognizable in his dramas, particularly in the tavern scenes that take place in Eastcheap in the *Henry IV* plays, but there are also references in *The Merry Wives of Windsor*, and in *Cymbeline* it is referred to as Lud's town, an old name for London.

Clarkenwell

Smy'the Fyeld

Bud well   *Blak freres*   *Benams Castle*   *Brokenworf*   *Quene hine*   *The Crane*

Parr's Garden

The Boull bay tyng.   *The Beare bayting*

LOTTERY

❡ IN ROMAN MYTHOLOGY, Fortuna is
the goddess of luck, fate and fortune. Depicted
with a ball or a wheel, her *rota fortunae* from
the original medieval concept, she was believed
to control the fortunes of men, their luck rising
and falling with the movements of the wheel and their
positions on it. Hamlet describes 'the slings and arrows of
outrageous fortune' that men must contend with, and in *As You Like
It* Celia wishes they could 'mock the good housewife Fortune from her
wheel, that her gifts may henceforth be bestowed equally'. In Rome,
and keen to know of his future chances, Antony asks a soothsayer
'whose fortunes shall rise higher: Caesar's or mine?' The soothsayer
bids him return to Egypt, to leave Caesar's side, and further warns:
'If thou dost play with him at any game / Thou art sure to lose;
and of that natural luck / He beats thee 'gainst the odds.'

In *The Merchant of Venice*, Nerissa reassures Portia that the
game, or lottery, she must play with her potential suitors will end
well. The odds, Nerissa believes, will be stacked in Portia's favour:

Your father was ever virtuous, and holy men at their death
have good inspirations; therefore the lottery that he hath
devised in these three chests of gold, silver, and lead, whereof
who chooses his meaning chooses you, will no doubt never be
chosen by any rightly but one who you shall rightly love.

The
Merchant
of Venice
1.2

Ill fortune and bad luck can drive men to desperate measures.
Macbeth's men tell him they have suffered 'the vile blows and buffets
of the world', and they are easily persuaded into murdering Banquo.
One of the men is 'reckless what I do to spite the world', the other
'so weary with disasters, tugged with Fortune, that I would set my
life on any chance to mend it or be rid on't.'

LOVERS

*Lovers and madmen have such seething brains,
Such shaping fantasies, that apprehend
More than cool reason ever comprehends.*

❡ LOVERS chase, woo, sigh, yearn, dote, bicker, suffer, kiss, cry
and – of course – love in Shakespeare's plays. The relationships
between Romeo and Juliet, Antony and Cleopatra, Beatrice and
Benedick, and Desdemona and Othello, amongst many others,
are played out across the comedies and tragedies alike. Love is a
recurring theme, the word 'love' is mentioned 1,640 times, and
the *Sonnets* are regarded as some of the finest love poems in the
English language.

   The madness, irrationality and magic of love are explored
through Helena, Hermia, Lysander and Demetrius, known collec-
tively as the lovers, in A *Midsummer Night's Dream*. A troublesome
love triangle at the play's opening becomes more complicated as
the lovers eventually find themselves all wandering in the moonlit
wood and the magical interventions of the Fairy King, Oberon, take
effect. Lysander had mused from the outset that 'the course of true
love never did run smooth', and to love, and to be loved, becomes
bewildering and inexplicable. Hermia, so sure of Lysander's affections, now finds him changed: 'Why are you grown so rude? What
change is this, / Sweet love?', and despite Demetrius's continual
spurning of Helena, she finds that pursuing him is almost beyond
her control, his magnetic pull too strong: 'Leave you your power to
draw, / And I shall have no power to follow you.'

   At the play's end Demetrius, too, cannot explain what has
happened or how it is that his affections have returned to Helena:
'But, my good lord, I wot not by what power – / But by some power
it is – my love to Hermia, / Melted as the snow.' Order is finally
restored and, upon discovering the lovers sound asleep, Theseus,

Duke of Athens, notes that they have reunited: 'Good morrow, friends. Saint Valentine is past. Begin these wood-birds but to couple now?' Traditionally birds were said to pair up on 14 February.

MERMAID

A
Midsummer
Night's
Dream
2.1

My gentle puck, come hither.
Thou rememb'rest
Since once I sat upon a promontory
And heard a mermaid
on a dolphin's back
Uttering such dulcet and
harmonious breath
That the rude sea grew civil at her song
And certain stars shot madly from
their spheres
To hear the sea-maid's music?

☛ THE MERMAID has been a figure of folklore since antiquity, a sea creature traditionally depicted as a young woman from the waist up with her lower half formed into a fish's tail. In Shakespeare's time, mermaids were often pictured holding mirrors and combing their hair, and, as such, were a symbol of vanity. The myth of the mermaid was perpetuated by sailors' mis-sightings at sea, although the legend of the beautiful sea-maiden enchanting seafarers with her song is indebted to the Sirens of Greek mythology.

This is the prevalent image in Shakespeare's works. In *Venus and Adonis*, Adonis steadfastly resists Venus's pleading, 'Bewitching like the wanton mermaid's songs', and in *The Comedy of Errors*, Antipholus of Syracuse is smitten by Luciana:

The Comedy
of Errors
3.2

O, train me not, sweet mermaid, with thy note
To drown me in thy sister's flood of tears.
Sing, siren, for thyself, and I will dote.
Spread o'er the silver waves thy golden hairs,
And as a bed I'll take them, and there lie...

Believing him to be his twin brother, her sister's husband, Luciana chastises him and, fearing he may have been enchanted, Antipholus declares 'I'll stop mine ears against the mermaid's song.'

But mermaids could also be benevolent. In *The Tempest*, Shakespeare invokes the friendly water spirits of brooks and springs: 'You nymphs, call'd Naiads, of the windring brooks, / With your sedged crowns and ever-harmless looks...' Similarly, the Nereids that accompany Cleopatra's barge of burnished gold are the sea nymphs of Classical mythology, who were often depicted riding on the back of a dolphin and were seen as the saviours of sailors and fishermen. Their protective nature is evoked in Gertrude's description of Ophelia drowning in the brook: 'Her clothes spread wide, / And mermaid-like a while they bore her up...'

MOON

...you may as well
Forbid the sea for to obey the moon...

The
Winter's
Tale
1.2

❡ GOVERNING THE NATURAL cycles of day and night, the tides and the seasons, the moon was believed in Shakespeare's time to be an important and influential celestial body.

In the opening scene of *A Midsummer Night's Dream*, Theseus and Hippolyta measure with reference to the moon the time until their wedding. With four days to wait until the new moon and

their 'nuptial hour', Theseus is frustrated: 'how slow this old moon wanes!' Hippolyta reassures him that 'Four days will quickly steep themselves in night, / Four nights will quickly dream away the time.' In the same play, the rift between the King and Queen of the Fairies is creating disharmony in nature, the unseasonable weather and 'contagious fogs' described by Titania all the result of the moon's anger: 'Therefore the moon, the governess of floods, / Pale in her anger washes all the air, / That rheumatic diseases do abound...'

Pocket-books of the period, called almanacs, encouraged Elizabethans to work in harmony with the natural world and included astronomical information and the phases of the moon along with weather forecasts, agricultural tips, advice for the home and important dates for fairs and holidays. The first printed almanac in English had appeared in 1497, and by the second half of the sixteenth century such books were popular bestsellers. As the amateur actors led by Bottom in *A Midsummer Night's Dream* rehearse, they consult an almanac to see if the moon will shine the night they perform in front of the newly married Theseus and Hippolyta. Bottom cries: 'A calendar, a calendar – look in the almanac, find out moonshine, find out moonshine;' Quince, with the book, replies 'Yes, it doth shine that night.'

In the tragedies the moon is an ominous influence. Juliet exclaims to Romeo at the start of their relationship, 'O swear not by the moon, th'inconstant moon, / That monthly changes in her circled orb,' fearful that his love for her might be as fleeting. In *Antony and Cleopatra*, Antony recognizes that his life in Egypt with Cleopatra is threatened: 'Alack, our terrene moon / Is now eclipsed, and it portends alone / The fall of Antony.' Later, as Cleopatra prepares to die, she is bold in her resolve and shuns the changeable moon: 'Now from head to foot / I am marble-constant. Now the fleeting moon / No planet is of mine.'

MULBERRY

Coriolanus
3.2
Now humble as the ripest mulberry
That will not hold the handling...

❡ THE MULBERRY is a fruit tree bearing white or dark-red berries. In his *Herball* of 1597, John Gerard observes that they 'grow plentifully in Italy and other hot regions, where they doe maintaine great woods and groves of them, that their Silke wormes may feed thereon'. Silkworms feed predominantly on the leaves of the white mulberry tree. The soft juicy berries of the black mulberry, although difficult to pick, were used to make syrups and preserves.

In *A Midsummer Night's Dream*, Titania instructs her fairy attendants to feed Bottom 'With purple grapes, green figs, and mulberries'. Later in the same play, the Mechanicals perform the Classical tale of Pyramus and Thisbe, in which the hero and heroine meet their cruel death in the shade of a mulberry tree. Pyramus discovers Thisbe's bloodstained mantle:

A
Midsummer
Night's
Dream
5.1
Whereat with blade — with bloody, blameful blade —
He bravely broached his boiling bloody breast;
And Thisbe, tarrying in mulberry shade,
His dagger drew and died.

In Ovid's *Metamorphoses*, Shakespeare's source for the Mechanicals' play, it is the spurting blood of the dying Pyramus that transforms the white mulberry tree, turning its berries red.

In 1607, James I instructed landowners to plant 10,000 mulberry trees to help establish an English silk industry. The trees imported to meet the demand were all, however, black mulberry trees rather than the white variety preferred by the silkworm. The Jacobean silk industry never took off, but the black mulberry tree was established in a number of English

gardens. The mulberry in the Great Garden at Shakespeare's New Place is said to have been grown from a cutting taken from a tree planted by Shakespeare himself, the original having been felled in the 1750s by the property's disgruntled owner and its wood turned into souvenirs for the burgeoning Shakespeare tourist industry.

MUSIC

❡ MUSIC was part of everyday life in Shakespeare's England at all levels of society, from the royal court to the tradespeople who 'keep such a-chanting and singing in their shops', as the author of *The Praise of Musicke* notes in 1586. At a time when people went to hear, as much as to see, a play, music was integral to the entertainment. Theatrical performances would sometimes end with a jig, and songs are woven into Shakespeare's plays, from the bawdy tavern songs in *Henry IV part 2* to the pitiful 'Willow Song' that Desdemona sings in *Othello*, foretelling her own fate.

Trumpet flourishes herald the arrival of kings on stage, and drums evoke the clamour of war. 'A flourish, trumpets! Strike alarum, drums!' calls the king in *Richard III*. Hautboys – forerunners of the modern oboe – produced an eerie, ominous sound, and were played, for example, to accompany the appearance of the witches in *Macbeth*. The theatre companies also had in their inventory bells, tambourines, sackbuts, citterns and viols – bowed instruments played between the legs.

In *Twelfth Night*, Sir Andrew Aguecheek 'plays o'th' viol-de-gamboys', a fashionable instrument of the day, and in *The Taming of the Shrew*, Kate receives lute lessons from Hortensio, with little success:

The Taming
of the
Shrew
2.1

'Why no, for she hath broke the lute to me.
I did but tell her she mistook her frets,
And bowed her hand to teach her fingering,
When, with a most impatient devilish spirit,
'Frets, call you these?' quoth she,
'I'll fume with them.'
And with that word she struck
me on the head,
And through the instrument
my pate made way…*

The lute was traditionally the instrument of lovers and, though injurious here to Hortensio, was believed usually to have healing properties. In *Henry VIII*, for example, Queen Katherine calls to

her lady-in-waiting: 'Take thy lute, wench. My soul grows sad with
troubles. / Sing, and disperse 'em, if thou canst.' This belief in the
powerful influence of music was underpinned by the Renaissance
concept of the music of the spheres, in which the movements of the
planets and other celestial bodies were believed to create a form
of universal harmony. Lorenzo evokes this idea in *The Merchant
of Venice* as he sits with his lover, Jessica, awaiting the musicians:

> *Here will we sit, and let the sounds of music*
> *Creep in our ears. Soft stillness and the night*
> *Become the touches of sweet harmony.*
> *Sit, Jessica. Look how the floor of heaven*
> *Is thick inlaid with patens of bright gold.*
> *There's not the smallest orb which thou behold'st*
> *But in his motion like an angel sings,*
> *Still choiring to the young-eyed cherubins.*

The
Merchant
of Venice 5.1

Luscinia
The Nightingale .

Tijeguacuparoara
Marggr.

NIGHTINGALE

 A SMALL BROWN SONGBIRD, celebrated for its beautiful voice, the nightingale has figured in literature since antiquity. Its song is both a herald of spring and the sound of night, and has been long associated with poetry, love and lament. In *The Two Gentlemen of Verona*, the nightingale mirrors Valentine's forlorn state: 'Here can I sit alone, unseen of any / And to the nightingale's complaining notes / Tune my distresses and record my woes.'

Wishing to prolong their first night together, Juliet appeals to Romeo: 'Wilt thou be gone? It is not yet near day / It was the nightingale, and not the lark, / That pierced the fear-full hollow of thine ear / Nightly she sings on yon pom'granate tree. / Believe me, love, it was the nightingale.'

In Sonnet 102, Shakespeare likens the poetry he has written – or not written – for his lover to the nightingale's song. The nightingale is a summer visitor to England and its song appreciated more for not being heard all the time: 'Our love was new and then but in the spring / When I was wont to greet it with my lays, / As Philomel in summer's front doth sing, / And stops her pipe in growth of riper days...'

Philomel is from the Greek for nightingale, hence the fairies in *A Midsummer Night's Dream* inviting the songbird to join them in lulling Titania to sleep:

> *Philomel with melody,*
> *Sing in our sweet lullaby;*
> *Lulla, lulla, lullaby; lulla, lulla, lullaby.*

A Midsummer Night's Dream 2.2

NOTHING

Hamlet
2.2 *Why, then 'tis none to you, for there is nothing
either good or bad but thinking makes it so.*

❡ IN SHAKESPEARE'S TIME, theatregoers went principally to hear a play, not to see it. The stage was relatively bare, with minimal scenery and props, and it was the words instead that conjured the scene, described the play's action and revealed the emotions of the characters. Creating something out of nothing relied on the imagination, calling for a 'muse of fire' as the Chorus does in *Henry V*. Famously, in the prologue, the Chorus encourages the audience to picture the scene, to 'think, when we talk of horses, that you see them', and to let the words on their 'imaginary forces work'. In *A Midsummer Night's Dream*, Theseus also muses on the power of the imagination. Reflecting on the strange tales he's heard from the lovers of their night spent in the woods, he believes them to be the invention of a poet. It is the poet, with an imagination that equals that of the lunatic and the lover, Oberon says, who 'bodies forth / The forms of things unknown' and then with his pen 'turns them to shapes, and gives to airy nothing / A local habitation and a name'. The exoticism of Cleopatra's Egypt, the brooding darkness of Macbeth's castle, the magic of Prospero's island, Richard III's ghosts at Bosworth Field and Hamlet's inner turmoil: all created out of nothing.

Shakespeare also plays with the meaning of the word 'nothing'. An ominous and loaded word, particularly in the tragedies, speaking of nothing becomes the catalyst for events with far-reaching and significant consequences. In *King Lear* Cordelia quietly and simply answers: 'Nothing, my lord,' in response to her father's challenging question: 'what can you say to draw / A third more opulent than your sisters? Speak,' and in *Othello* Iago plants the seeds of fatal jealousy by implying there is more to Cassio and Desdemona's

> ## *Cor.* Nothing my Lord.
> ## *Lear.* Nothing?

relationship than there is. 'What doſt thou say?' asks Othello, to which Iago replies 'Nothing, my lord. Or if, I know not what.' In *Hamlet*, Hamlet, unaware of the plot to poison him, agrees to take part in the proposed duel with Laertes. He believes he has nothing to lose: 'I will win for him an I can. If not, I'll gain nothing but my shame and the odd hits.' Poignantly, the audience knows he ſtands to lose everything.

In the comedy *Much Ado About Nothing*, as the play's name suggeſts, all ends happily, the wit and humour throughout moſt of the action, and the comic antics of Dogberry, offsetting the malicious scheme set in motion by Don John to ruin Hero's happiness. Even in this play, though, nothing can ſtill carry weight. Having teased and argued with each other from the outset, it is only towards the end of the play that Beatrice and Benedick finally begin to realize fully their love for each other. 'I do love nothing in the world so well as you. Is not that ſtrange?' asks Benedick. Beatrice, equally hesitant, replies: 'It were as possible for me to say I loved nothing so well as you, but believe me not, and yet I lie not. I confess nothing nor I deny nothing.' By opting to talk of or admit nothing, both are in fact saying everything.

Much adoe about Nothing.

Actus primus, Scena prima.

NUTMEG

Henry V
3.7

*He's of the colour
of the nutmeg.*

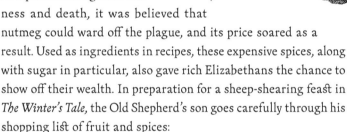

❡ IMPORTED FROM THE NEW WORLD during the Tudor period, nutmeg was a popular and increasingly valuable spice alongside cinnamon, pepper and ginger. Used in pomanders (balls filled with perfumes, waxes and spices) that were carried as a protection against sickness and death, it was believed that nutmeg could ward off the plague, and its price soared as a result. Used as ingredients in recipes, these expensive spices, along with sugar in particular, also gave rich Elizabethans the chance to show off their wealth. In preparation for a sheep-shearing feast in *The Winter's Tale*, the Old Shepherd's son goes carefully through his shopping list of fruit and spices:

The Winter's
Tale
4.3

*I must have saffron to colour the warden pies; mace; dates,
none — that's out of my note; nutmegs, seven; a race or two
of ginger — but that I may beg; four pounds of prunes,
and as many of raisins o'th' sun.*

Warden pies take their name from the warden pear, an old variety of the fruit first cultivated in the thirteenth century. A popular dish in Shakespeare's time, the sweet pie was flavoured with spices exactly as the Old Shepherd's son describes.

OAK

☞ A SYMBOL OF STRENGTH and survival for centuries, oak trees have a long tradition within English myth and folklore, and numerous associations with royalty. Queen Elizabeth's Oak in Greenwich Park has been dead for more than one hundred years but is believed to have been on the site since the twelfth century, and to be the tree that the young Elizabeth I picnicked under. Ancient kings wore crowns of oak leaves and Shakespeare makes reference to the crown of leaves given to Roman citizens for saving the life of a fellow citizen in *Coriolanus*. Talking proudly of her soldier son, Volumnia describes how 'To a cruel war I sent him, from whence he returned his brows bound with oak.' More famously, Shakespeare weaves the story of Herne the hunter and Herne's Oak into the plot of *The Merry Wives of Windsor*. In folklore, Herne is said to haunt Windsor Forest and Great Park, tormenting the cattle and rattling chains. Tricked by the wives into disguising himself as Herne by wearing a stag's horns, Falstaff makes his way to Herne's Oak at midnight, where he believes he will secretly meet with both women: 'There is an old tale goes that Herne the hunter / Sometime a keeper here in Windsor Forest / Doth all the winter time at still midnight / Walk around about an oak with great ragg'd horns...'

Oak is one of the hardest and most durable timbers, and was used in shipbuilding right up until the mid-nineteenth century. It was also the wood used to build the Globe theatre in London in 1599.

OVID

*...for the elegance, facility, and golden cadence
of poesy — caret. Ovidius Naso was the man.*

¶ OVID WAS A ROMAN POET whose works were hugely
influential on English literature during the Renaissance. His most
celebrated work was *Metamorphoses*, a collection of stories of Classical
mythology, featuring the tales of Daedalus and Icarus, Echo and
Narcissus, Pyramus and Thisbe, among many others. Shakespeare
would have been familiar with Ovid's work in the original Latin
from school and had read Arthur Golding's English translation
of *Metamorphoses*, first published in 1567. Most of Shakespeare's
Classical references are indebted to Ovid, and Prospero's line in
The Tempest, 'Ye elves of hills, brooks, standing lakes and groves,'
is almost a direct lift from Golding's text.

Ovid's brief account of Venus and Adonis's story is reworked
by Shakespeare into the exquisite narrative poem *Venus and Adonis*,
and the original Ovidian tale of Philomel, who is raped and has
her tongue cut out by her sister's husband, Terceus, is echoed by
Shakespeare in the violation of Lavinia in *Titus Andronicus*. Later
in the same play, it is a copy of *Metamorphoses* that helps Lavinia
to communicate her ordeal:

Titus: Lucius, what book is that she tosseth so?
Young Lucius: Grandsire, 'tis Ovid's Metamorphoses.
My mother gave it me....
Titus: Soft, so busily she turns the leaves.
Help her. What would she find? Lavinia, shall I read?
This is the tragic tale of Philomel,
And treats of Tereus' treason and his rape,
And rape, I fear, was root of thy annoy.

OWL

❡ THE OWL is a nocturnal hunting bird, 'night's herald' or 'the nightly owl', with large 'staring' eyes and an acute sense of vision. The little owl, especially, is associated with the Greek goddess of wisdom, Athene, and the owl has been a symbol of wisdom since ancient times. But it is also believed to be a bird of ill-omen. In *Julius Caesar*, the owl's appearance during the daytime is a portent for Casca of events to come:

Julius
Caesar
1.3

And yesterday the bird of night did sit
Even at noonday upon the market-place,
Hooting and shrieking.

Owls were also believed to foretell death. Lady Macbeth, having drugged King Duncan's guards, is unnerved by an owl's ominous call: 'Hark, peace! – It was the owl that shrieked, the fatal bellman / Which gives the stern'st good-night.' Macbeth kills Duncan and the following morning Lennox reports 'strange screams of death' and how 'the obscure bird clamoured the livelong night'. Owls usually hunt at low level but the natural order is turned on its head and Macbeth's assassination of the king is as if 'A falcon, tow'ring in her pride of place, / Was by a mousing owl hawked at and killed.'

Only in *Love's Labour's Lost* does Shakespeare represent the owl in a positive light. The song of Winter echoes with the call of the tawny owl: 'Tu-whit, tu-whoo! – A merry note.'

PLAGUE

 PLAGUE had been endemic in England since the fourteenth century. Transmitted by infected fleas from the black rat, it was fatal and fast-spreading. Symptoms included fever, swellings and sores, as reflected in King Lear's railing at his daughter Goneril:

> *Thou art a boil,*
> *A plague-sore or embossèd carbuncle*
> *In my corrupted blood.*

King Lear
2.2

An outbreak of the bubonic plague hit Stratford-upon-Avon in the year Shakespeare was born, an entry in the parish register for 11 July 1564 recording its arrival in the town: *'Hic incipit pestis'* ('here begins the plague'). Shakespeare was lucky to survive. The epidemic claimed over 200 lives – around one-sixth of the town's population – including four children in Shakespeare's street. It is feasible Shakespeare would have been taken out of town to the safety of his grandparents' farm in nearby Wilmcote. The Tudors believed that the disease was airborne, and that good air prevented infection. Similarly, fresh herbs and sweet-smelling pomanders were used to combat the plague. Shakespeare has this idea in mind when Venus tells Adonis that his sweet lips will:

> *drive infection from the dangerous year,*
> *That the star-gazers, having writ on death,*
> *May say the plague is banished by thy breath!*

Venus
and Adonis
508-10

Venus and Adonis was published in 1593 and most likely written in 1592, the 'dangerous year' when an epidemic hit London and wiped out around one-fifth of its population. Believing the plague could be transmitted directly from person to person, and to prevent it spreading quickly wherever large crowds gathered, the authorities closed the playhouses. A further epidemic in the summer of 1603 kept the new King James I out of the capital, and his coronation was deferred until the following year.

To contain the plague during an epidemic, sufferers were often quarantined and the door of their house marked with a cross. In *The Two Gentlemen of Verona*, Speed remarks that Valentine walked 'alone, like one that had the pestilence' and, in *Romeo and Juliet*, Friar John explains that he had not delivered a vital letter to Romeo because: 'the searchers of the town / Suspecting that we both were in a house / Where the infectious pestilence did reign / Sealed up the doors, and would not let us forth…'

Plague and pestilence are most often encountered in Shakespeare's plays as apparently 'mere' insults or curses. The historic context, however, gives a potent currency to Mercutio's dying curse, 'A plague o' both your houses.'

ORDERS,
thought meete by his Maieftie, and his Priuie Counfell, to be
executed throughout the Counties of this
Realme, in fuch Townes, Villages, and other
places, as are, or may be hereafter infected with the Plague, for the
ftay of further increafe
of the fame.

Alfo, an Aduife fet downe by the beft
learned in Phyficke within this Realme,
containing fundry good Rules and eafie Medicines without charge to the meaner fort of people,
afwel for the prefuration of his good Sub-
iects from the plague before Infection, as for the curing and orde-
ring of them after they
fhalbe infected.

PORTRAIT

¶ IN TUDOR ENGLAND only the rich and wealthy could afford to commission a portrait. Demonstrating the sitter's status and wealth, or power, the objects included in the painting were often significant or symbolic and the sitter wore his or her most expensive clothes. Portraits of Elizabeth I used elaborate symbolism to celebrate and flatter her, emphasizing her position as the Virgin Queen. Portrait miniatures were popular and these tiny, detailed images encased in a locket were given as intimate gifts. In *Twelfth Night* Olivia hands the disguised Viola a locket as a token of her affection: 'Here, wear this jewel for me, 'tis my picture.' Portraits appeared in books of the period, too; specially commissioned engravings for collected works or important volumes that appeared on the title pages, or frontispieces. The most iconic image of Shakespeare appears on the title page of the First Folio. Engraved by Martin Droeshout, it is unclear which was the original source painting or drawing, though Shakespeare's friend Ben Jonson, in his poem that appears on the page facing the portrait, makes clear that the likeness is a good one:

> *This Figure, that thou here seest put,*
> *It was for gentle Shakespeare cut;*
> *Wherein the Graver had a strife*
> *With Nature, to out-doo the life:*
> *O, could he but have drawne his wit*
> *As well in brasse, as he hath hit*
> *His face; the Print would then surpasse*
> *All, that was ever writ in brasse.*
> *But, since he cannot, Reader, looke*
> *Not on his Picture, but his Booke.*

Ben Jonson, 'To the Reader', in the First Folio

Mr. WILLIAM

SHAKESPEARES

COMEDIES,
HISTORIES, &
TRAGEDIES.

Published according to the True Originall Copies.

Gentle Maister Shakespear

Martin Droeshout sculpsit London.

LONDON
Printed by Isaac Iaggard, and Ed. Blount. 1623.

PRINTING

I warrant he hath a thousand of these letters, writ with blank space for different names — sure, more, and these are of the second edition. He will print them, out of doubt...

The Merry
Wives of
Windsor
2.1

❡ IN 1604, SHAKESPEARE'S contemporary the dramatist John Marston wrote that it afflicted him 'to think that scenes, invented merely to be spoken, should be enforcively published to read'. It was the acting companies that owned the plays, however, and they would often sell the publishing rights to generate funds or renew interest in their repertoire. Nineteen of Shakespeare's plays were printed as quartos while he was still alive, some running into numerous editions. Shakespeare's first work to appear in print was in fact not a play but the narrative poem *Venus and Adonis*. The first edition was printed and published by Richard Field in 1593, who would also subsequently print the first editions of *The Rape of Lucrece* and the poem *The Phoenix and the Turtle*. Field was originally from Stratford-upon-Avon and would have known Shakespeare well.

It was unusual to be both the printer and publisher. Having acquired the manuscript, a publisher would usually commission a master printer to produce the book for him to sell either wholesale or in his own bookshop, as advertised on the title page of the book. The title page to *Venus and Adonis*, for example, reads 'Imprinted by Richard Field, and are to be sold at the sign of the white Greyhound in Paules Church-yard', the area around St Paul's Cathedral being the home of London's bookselling community.

In the printing house, a compositor created a block of metal type letter by letter, from two cases ſtationed in front of him, the upper case containing the capital letters and the lower case for the reſt. Each line was set in a composing ſtick and then transferred into a wooden tray, known as a galley, until the page was completed. The pages to be printed onto one sheet of paper were held together in an iron frame, ready to be inked. While one pressman inked the type, a second prepared a dampened sheet of paper on a wooden frame, called a tympan, which was then lowered onto the type and pressed under a metal plate to create an impression. Once printed, the metal type was returned to its cases. The second side of the sheet could be printed the same day, and in this way, an edition of a book created in a couple of weeks.

The capital letters.

A B C D E F G H I K L M N O P Q R S T
V X Y Z &.

A B C D E F G H I J K L M N O P Q R S T
U V X Y Z.

The ſmall letters.

a b c d e f g h i j k l m n o p q r ſ s t u v x y z.
a b c d e f g h i j k l m n o p q r ſ s t u v x y z.

QUEEN
ELIZABETH I

Heaven, from thy endless goodness
send prosperous life, long, and
ever happy, to the high and mighty
Princess of England, Elizabeth.

Henry VIII
(All Is True)
5.4

☞ DAUGHTER OF KING HENRY VIII (1491–1547) and
his second wife Anne Boleyn (1507–1536), Elizabeth was born in
September 1533 and became Queen of England and Ireland in 1558.
The last of the Tudor monarchs, Elizabeth was well educated and
fluent in several languages and is said to have had sound political
judgement, surrounding herself with well-chosen ministers and
advisors. Under her rule, the English Renaissance reached its peak,
with architecture, music, the visual arts, literature and the theatre
all flourishing. As chief writer with the playing company The Lord
Chamberlain's Men, Shakespeare, along with his fellow actors,
is known to have performed at court before Elizabeth on several

occasions. Two comedies were performed at Greenwich Palace during the Christmas period in 1594, and *Love's Labour's Lost* was performed at Christmas 1597 at Whitehall. Legend has it that the Queen was particularly fond of the character Falstaff, who first appeared in the *Henry IV* plays, and wanted to see him in love, but although *The Merry Wives of Windsor* was performed at court, it cannot be proved that Shakespeare wrote it especially for Queen Elizabeth. Her birth and legacy are, however, celebrated in the play *The Famous History of the Life of King Henry the Eighth*, or *All Is True* as it was first known. Written by Shakespeare and his contemporary John Fletcher in 1613, the final scene foretells the glory of her reign. Speaking over the child at her christening, the Archbishop of Canterbury predicts:

Henry VIII
(All Is True)
5.4

This royal infant — heaven still move about her —
Though in her cradle, yet now promises
Upon this land a thousand thousand blessings
Which time shall bring to ripeness.

QUESTION

Macbeth
2.3

Knock, knock, knock. Who's there, i'th' name of Beelzebub?
Here's a farmer that hanged himself on th'expectation
of plenty...

❡ FROM THE FIRST recorded 'knock, knock' joke, told by the porter in *Macbeth*, to some of the most memorable lines in the English language, Shakespeare uses questions as dramatic and rhetorical devices throughout his poems and plays.

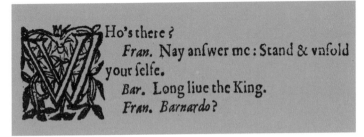

Ho's there?
Fran. Nay anſwer me : Stand & vnfold
your ſelfe.
Bar. Long liue the King.
Fran. Barnardo?

The very firſt line of *Hamlet* is 'Who's there?', spoken by the
sentinel Barnardo, and in a play that is full of queſtions, Barnardo's
opening words immediately create a sense of anticipation and
imagined possibilities. In the next scene, Hamlet queſtions Barnardo
and Marcellus about the ghoſt of his father and wants to hear every
detail as he seeks to make sense, in a rapid exchange, of what they
have seen: 'Armed say you? / Armed, my lord. / From top to toe? /
My lord from head to foot.' Seeing the ghoſt for himself, Hamlet
declares: 'Be thy intents wicked or charitable, / Thou com'ſt in such
a queſtionable shape / That I will speak to thee.' Hamlet wants to
know 'why is this? Wherefore? What should we do?' and, as the ghoſt
reveals the ſtory of his murder, Hamlet's queſtions punctuate the
scene to dramatic effect: 'What?', 'Murder?', 'Mine uncle?'

It is Hamlet too who asks the moſt famous queſtion in all of
Shakespeare's plays:

> *To be, or not to be; that is the question:*
> *...To die, to sleep.*
> *To sleep, perchance to dream. Ay, there's the rub,*
> *For in that sleep of death what dreams may come*
> *When we have shuffled off this mortal coil*
> *Must give us pause.*

Hamlet
3.1

? ?

Hamlet's speech, in which he deliberates taking his own life and wrestles with the imagined possibilities of death, is an example of a soliloquy, a moment in the play when a character, seemingly alone on stage, shares his or her private thoughts with the audience. In soliloquies, the character's conflicting doubts or desires are often played out through questions. An example is Macbeth contemplating the assassination of the king in *Macbeth*: 'Is this a dagger which I see before me, / The handle toward my hand?' Another is the opening line of Juliet's soliloquy in *Romeo and Juliet*: 'O Romeo, Romeo, wherefore art thou Romeo?'

Shylock uses rhetorical questions to advance his justification for revenge in *The Merchant of Venice*. 'Hath not a Jew eyes?' he asks Salerio, suggesting that Jews and Christians are just alike:

The
Merchant
of Venice
3.1

> *If you prick us do we not bleed? If you tickle us do we not laugh? If you poison us do we not die? And if you wrong us shall we not revenge? If we are like you in the rest, we will resemble you in that.*

Shakespeare also uses questions to set up the persuasive argument of many of his sonnets, most famously the first line of sonnet 18, in which the poet speaks to the reader directly: 'Shall I compare thee to a summer's day? / Thou art more lovely and more temperate.' Perhaps it is because questions have this power to connect directly with the reader – and with an audience on stage – that Shakespeare's questions resonate with us so strongly.

Ham. To be, or not to be, that is the Question:

QUILL

Her maid is gone, and she prepares to write,
First hovering o'er the paper with her quill.

❡ THE QUILL PEN was used as a writing instrument until the
nineteenth century. In Shakespeare's time the preference was for
a quill crafted from goose or raven feathers. The quill was shaped
using a penknife to cut the nib and to shave the feathers from
the lower part of the pen. The nib would be refashioned as the
quill wore down, until a new pen was needed. Penmanship was
an important skill and the art of preparing a pen as much a part
of it as handwriting.

The Rape of Lucrece 1296-97

In the sixteenth century, there were two common styles of
handwriting: secretary hand and italic. The surviving copies of
Shakespeare's signature show that he wrote in secretary hand, a
style of writing designed for fluency and speed. According to Martin
Billingsley in *The Pens Excellencie or the Secretaries Delighte* (1618),
it was so called 'partly because it is the Secretaries common hand,
and partly also, because it is the onely vsuall hand of England, for
dispatching of all manner of businesses for the most part'. Some
of the letter forms were different from those we use now and their
shapes less fixed. The letters i and j and u and v were interchangeable,
spelling was more fluid and often included abbreviations.

Much closer in appearance to modern printed text, the italic
style, as its name suggests, had been introduced from Italy and was
popular with scholars and the Tudor court. Elizabeth I, for example,
was taught it as a child. In *Twelfth Night* Malvolio believes it is
Olivia's italic handwriting he recognizes in the letter he discovers:

By my life this is my lady's hand. These be her very c's,
her u's, and her t's, and thus makes she her great P's.
It is in contempt of question her hand.

Twelfth Night 2.5

REMEMBRANCE

Adieu, adieu, Hamlet. Remember me.

☞ SO BIDS THE GHOST of Hamlet's father after recounting his horrible death at his own brother's hand. Hamlet, grief-stricken and appalled, vows: 'thy commandment all alone shall live / Within the book and volume of my brain / Unmixed with baser matter.' To avenge his father and honour his memory, Hamlet swears that his murdering uncle, Claudius, will be held to account: 'Now to my word: / It is 'Adieu, adieu, remember me'. / I have sworn't.' Claudius, it turns out, will not forget Hamlet either.

In *Twelfth Night*, too, the Countess Olivia has devoted herself to mourning and remembering. Valentine, an attendant of Orsino's sent with messages to Olivia, explains when denied admittance to her home, why he could not see her:

> *But like a cloistress she will veilèd walk*
> *And water once a day her chamber round*
> *With eye-offending brine — all this to season*
> *A brother's dead love, which she would keep fresh*
> *And lasting in her sad remembrance.*

Olivia's salty tears, it would seem, are helping to preserve her memories.

In Shakespeare's time, rosemary, an attractive and aromatic herb with needle-like leaves and blue or purple flowers, symbolized remembrance, fidelity and friendship. It was traditionally carried by mourners at a funeral, and sometimes scattered into the grave, and the herb was also dipped into scented water and wound into bridal wreaths. In *The Winter's Tale*, Perdita hands out rue and rosemary to honour her guests with 'grace and remembrance'. The scent and appearance of both, she tells them, will keep 'all the winter long'. In *Hamlet*, the troubled Ophelia states it simply: 'There's rosemary, that's for remembrance. Pray, love, remember.' Today, some people wear a sprig of rosemary on 23 April to remember Shakespeare on the anniversary of his death.

RINGS

Look how my ring encompasseth thy finger;
Even so thy breast encloseth my poor heart.
Wear both of them, for both of them are thine.

Richard III
1.2

❡ JEWELLERY WAS POPULAR in Tudor England and there was something to suit every budget. Semi-precious stones, such as turquoise, carnelian, onyx and jasper were carved for cameos or used as beads. Rubies, emeralds, sapphires, opals, garnets and pearls were used in necklaces, pendants, brooches, earrings – and rings. Worn by both men and women, on every finger and sometimes the thumb, rings were usually made from gold or silver, though they could also be made with cheaper, base metals. The gemstones

used were frequently selected for their supposed healing powers or protective qualities, and thus the ring became more significant to the wearer. Gemstones, like the herbs and flowers used by doctors, housewives and apothecaries, were believed to have positive and healing properties, just as the Friar in *Romeo and Juliet* describes: 'O mickle is the powerful grace that lies / In plants, herbs, stones, and their true qualities.'

Rings were worn for protection but also to represent love, commitment and marriage. Both gimmel rings – a hoop that split into two, sometimes three parts, and concealed a heart beneath clasped hands – and posy rings, with verse inscribed within the hoop, were popular choices for wedding bands. For remembrance, memorial or *memento mori* ('Remember you must die') rings featured the name, or initials, of the deceased and his or her lifedates. In his own will, Shakespeare left 26s 8d (around £1.38p) each to seven of his friends, including John Heminges, Henry Condell and Richard Burbage, so that they might buy rings in remembrance of him.

Rings are important to the action in a number of Shakespeare's plays. In *All's Well That Ends Well*, Helena is determined to marry the proud and disdainful Bertram, and takes up his challenge that in order for him to accept her as his wife, she must take a ring from his finger and become pregnant with his child. When Helena outwits him and accomplishes both of these things, the ring becomes symbolic of the promise he made to marry her. In *The Merchant of Venice*, Bassanio and Graziano are tested by their wives, persuaded by Portia and Nerissa (disguised as men) into handing over their rings. Bassanio is at first reluctant: 'Good sir, this ring was given me by my wife, / And when she put it on she made me vow / That I should neither sell, nor give, nor lose it,'– but he does part with it. Graziano also hands over his ring, one he later describes as 'a hoop of gold, a paltry ring,' before Nerissa challenges him: 'What talk you of the posy or the value? / You swore to me when I did give it you / That you would wear it till your hour of death.'

Rings are also significant as a means of recognition and authentication. Signet rings, from the old French *signe* meaning to mark, were worn on the little finger or thumb and used to mark the wearer's initials in a wax seal on letters and documents. 'Look you, sir, here is the hand and seal of the Duke. You know the character, I doubt not, and the signet is not strange to you?' says the disguised Duke of Vienna in *Measure for Measure*. In *Henry IV part 1*, Falstaff laments the loss of his grandfather's ring: 'I have lost a seal-ring of my grandfather's worth forty mark.' A gold signet ring found in the grounds next to Holy Trinity Church in Stratford-upon-Avon on 16 March 1810 was a tantalizing discovery. Bearing the initials WS and intricate knotwork designs, the ring is believed by many to have been owned and used by Shakespeare himself.

Romeo
and Juliet
2.1

ROSE

What's in a name? That which
we call a rose
By any other word would smell as sweet.

❡ A FAVOURITE IN GARDENS of the period, the rose was used throughout the home, in herbal remedies, in cosmetics and in the kitchen. Celebrated for their colour and scent, and long associated with love, roses are the most-mentioned flower in Shakespeare's plays. Roses were also closely linked with Elizabeth I, through her persona as the Virgin Queen and with her royal heritage: the House of Tudor, founded by her grandfather Henry VII in 1485, took as its heraldic symbol the red-and-white Tudor rose. Combining the white rose of the House of York and the red rose of the House of Lancaster, the Tudor rose symbolized the union of the two lineages and an end to the thirty-two-years long War of the Roses.

In a fictional scene in *Henry VI part 1*, Shakespeare has the characters demonstrate their allegiances symbolically by picking the roses from the briars in the Temple garden. Richard Plantagenet selects a white rose and encourages the other gentlemen to follow suit; Somerset counters and plucks a red bloom:

Henry VI
part 1
2.4

> *Richard Plantagenet: Let him*
> *that is a true-born gentleman*
> *And stands upon the honour of his birth,*
> *If he suppose that I have pleaded truth,*
> *From off this briar pluck a white rose with me.*
> *Somerset: Let him that is no coward nor no flatterer,*
> *But dare maintain the party of the truth,*
> *Pluck a red rose from off this thorn with me.*

The opposing factions established, the Earl of Warwick prophesies the bloodshed to come: 'between the red rose and the white, / A thousand souls to death and deadly night.'

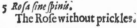

5 *Rosa sine spinis.*
The Rose without prickles.

white Rose; the especiall difference consi-
steth in the colour and smell of the floures;
for these are of a pale red colour, and of a
more pleasant smell, and fitter for meate or
medicine.

4 The *Rosa Provincialis minor*, or lesser
Prouince Rose differeth not from the former,
but is altogether lesser: the floures and fruit
are like: the vse in physick also agreeth with
the precedent.

5 The Rose without prickles hath many
young shootes comming from the root, di-
uiding themselues into diuers branches,
tongh, and of a woody substance as are all the
rest of the Roses, of the hight of two or three
cubites, smooth and plaine without any
roughnesse or prickles at all; whereon do
grow leaues like those of the Holland Rose,
of a shining deepe greene colour on the vp-
per side, vnderneath somewhat hoirie and
hairy. The floures grow at the toppes of the
branches, consisting of an infinite number of
leaues, greater than those of the Damaske
Rose, more double, and of a colour betweene
the Red and Damaske Roses, of a most sweet
smell. The fruit is round, red when it is ripe,
and stuffed with the like flockes and seeds of
those of the Damask Rose. The root is great,
wooddie, and far spreading.

SCHOOL

👉 CHILDREN ATTENDED PETTY SCHOOL between the ages of five and seven. From the French *petit*, meaning little, petty school offered young children an elementary education and usually took place in the home of a well-educated housewife or tradesperson. Children would learn to read and pronounce English with the aid of a hornbook, a printed sheet of paper mounted in a wooden frame behind a translucent layer of horn. The hornbook included the alphabet, vowel and consonant sounds, as well as a short prayer. In *Love's Labour's Lost*, Moth remarks that the Latin-spouting Holofernes 'teaches boys the horn-book', and in *King John*, Philip recalls the hornbook's ABC and the call and response of the catechism by which young children were taught the doctrine of the church:

King John
1.1

'I shall beseech you——'. That is Question now;
And then comes Answer like an Absey book.
'O sir,' says Answer, 'at your best command...

Some children, principally boys, went on to grammar school, and Shakespeare would have attended the King's New School above the guildhall in Stratford-upon-Avon. Here, with forty other boys, he would have learnt Latin grammar and rhetoric, and studied literature in Latin, including the plays of Terence and Plautus and the poetry of Ovid and Horace. In *Titus Andronicus*, Chiron recognizes two lines of Latin verse from a standard school textbook: 'O, 'tis a verse in Horace, I know it well. / I read it in the grammar long ago.'

There were few holidays and the school day was long, beginning at around 6 a.m. Hence, in *As You Like It*, Shakespeare's description of 'the whining schoolboy, with his satchel / And shining morning face, creeping like snail / Unwillingly to school.'

Boys attended school until the age of fourteen, before going on to university or to serve an apprenticeship. Some grammar schools, although very rarely, admitted girls in the lower forms, and wealthy families also would continue their daughter's formal education with a private schoolmaster, a privilege that Bianca enjoys in *The Taming of the Shrew*:

> *I am no breeching scholar in the schools.*
> *I'll not be tied to hours nor 'pointed times,*
> *But learn my lessons as I please myself...*

The Taming of the Shrew
3.1

Letters are divided into vowels and consonants.

A vowel is a letter, which maketh a full and perfect sound of it self. And there are five in number: namely, *a, e, i, o, u*; whereunto is added the Greek vowel *y*.
A consonant is a letter, which must needs be founded with a vowel; as, *b* with *e*. And all the letters, except the vowels, are consonants.

SHIP

Pericles
Scene 10

So up and down the poor ship drives.

¶ ELIZABETHAN ENGLAND was a maritime nation and ships
were the means by which new worlds were discovered, goods were
traded and enemies defeated. Ships feature in many of Shakespeare's
plays, both as plot devices and symbolically, and Shakespeare often
uses naval and nautical terms. Characters travel by ship and their
fortunes are shaped by the sea. In *The Merchant of Venice*, Antonio
'hath a ship of rich lading wracked on the narrow seas', leaving him
bankrupt and indebted to Shylock, and Hamlet's life is saved when
the ship that is carrying him to his death in England is captured
by pirates. Shipwrecks are a disruptive and transformative plot
device in *Twelfth Night*, *Pericles* and *The Comedy of Errors* and most
spectacularly in the opening scene of *The Tempest*:

The
Tempest
1.2

If by your art, my dearest father, you have
Put the wild waters in this roar, allay them.
The sky, it seems, would pour down stinking pitch,
But that the sea, mounting to th' welkin's cheek,
Dashes the fire out...A brave vessel...
Dashed all to pieces! O, the cry did knock
Against my very heart! Poor souls, they perished.

As a playwright, Shakespeare would have understood how immediately he could immerse and transport an audience by beginning a play with a storm at sea and the threat of shipwreck. Voyages at sea were perilous, and tempest-tossed ships are a recurring symbol of life's emotional journey. In *Timon of Athens,* the eponymous hero imagines 'nature's fragile vessel' in the throes of 'life's uncertain voyage', and in *Julius Caesar* Shakespeare evokes both the ambitious optimism and precarious nature of this maritime age in Brutus's call to action:

> *There is a tide in the affairs of men*
> *Which, taken at the flood, leads on to fortune;*
> *Omitted, all the voyage of their life*
> *Is bound in shallows and in miseries.*
> *On such a full sea are we now afloat,*
> *And we must take the current when it serves,*
> *Or lose our ventures.*

Julius Caesar 4.2

SPIDER

❡ SPIDERS were widely used in medical remedies during Shakespeare's time, despite the common belief that they were poisonous and associated with other unpleasant creatures, such as toads and adders. Amongst many other strange ingredients for remedies, including earthworm, snail, viper flesh and frogspawn, Dr John Hall (Shakespeare's son-in-law) mentions *aranearum telae* (spider web) in his patient notes as beneficial in the treatment of fevers. In folklore, spider webs were also said to help heal cuts and wounds, a practice to which Bottom makes reference on meeting the fairy called Cobweb in *A Midsummer Night's Dream*: 'I shall desire you of more acquaintance, good Master Cobweb. If I cut my finger, I shall make bold with you.' The English naturalist and physician Thomas Muffet (1563–1604) had a particular interest in spiders and their uses in medicine, writing fondly of them and the moral example he believed they set to man in the book *Theatrum Insectorum* (published in 1634).

In Shakespeare's plays, however, 'weaving spiders' and 'long legged spinners' are mentioned primarily for the webs and traps they create. The devious and unscrupulous Richard III is likened to a spider throughout the play, his murderous scheming and plotting all part of his 'deadly web'. Richard is a 'bottled spider' and not to be trusted, as Queen Elizabeth realizes towards the end of the play. Remembering Queen Margaret's earlier warnings, she laments:

Richard III
4.4

> *O thou didst prophesy the time would come*
> *That I should wish for thee to help me curse*
> *That bottled spider, that foul bunch-backed toad.*

Tab. xv

Scorpiones Terrestres Mouf

Sc. Aldr.

Aranei Spinnen Mouf

Ar. telaris sylv.

Arratiardio domest

Mouf. Ar. telaris supin prou 9

Ar. Lup 9 minim 9 Maxim 9 Mediocris

Ar. Longipes sylv.

Aranei Spinnen Aldrov. Tab. 1.

Tab. 2.

TENNIS

☞ TENNIS was a popular sport among the nobility in the sixteenth and seventeenth centuries, originating in France, where it was known as *Tenez*, French for 'take it', after the call made by players as they passed the ball over the net. Played by Henry VIII and watched by Queen Elizabeth I, tennis was played in an enclosed court, with the surrounding walls, open gallery and its sloping roof all part of the playing area. The balls were solid and often stuffed with hair, hence Claudio's jibe at Benedick that 'the barber's man hath been seen with him, and the old ornament of his cheek hath already stuffed tennis-balls.' In *Hamlet* Polonius refers to 'falling out at tennis', and in *Henry V* the French dauphin sends Henry a disparaging gift of tennis balls, provoking the king to respond:

Henry V
1.2

> When we have matched our rackets to these balls,
> We will in France, by God's grace, play a set
> Shall strike his father's crown into the hazard.
> Tell him he hath made a match with such a wrangler
> That all the courts of France will be disturbed
> With chases.

The hazard was the receiving end of the tennis court and the chase an additional opportunity to score at the end of each game by landing the ball past a designated mark in the opponent's court.

Writing in 1607, James Cleland cautions young noblemen against railing 'at the Tennis-keeper's score' or over-exerting themselves on court; 'Neverthelesse, I approve not those, who are ever in the

Tennis Court like Nackets, and heat themselves so much, that they rather breed, then expel sicknes.' Along with archery and bowling, tennis was considered suitable physical recreation for a gentleman. Football, in contrast, was an unruly mob game, played in the street and banned during Shakespeare's lifetime. In *King Lear*, the Earl of Kent insults Oswald, calling him a 'base football player'.

TIME

¶ THE ELIZABETHANS and Jacobeans were acutely aware of the passage of time and Shakespeare's works abound with references to time and the methods by which it was marked. In the sonnets, for example, time is a 'bloody tyrant', 'swift-footed' and 'devouring', to be defied only by the 'eternal lines' of poetry or, as the poem suggests, through procreation: 'And nothing 'gainst time's scythe can make defence / Save breed to brave him when he takes thee hence.' Time was often depicted as a figure holding a scythe. When the 'lovely boy' of sonnet 126 is said to hold in his power 'time's fickle glass, his sickle-hour', the allusion is to an hourglass, decorated with an emblematic sickle or scythe. The hourglass would measure time by the flow of sand. The sand enclosed in the top half of the glass would take an hour to run through, after which the glass was turned over to start again. Prospero uses this measurement literally in *The Tempest*, suggesting it is 'At least two glasses' past noon, but for Richard Plantagenet in *Henry VI part 3* it is symbolic of his whole existence, as he observes 'The sands are numbered that makes up my life.'

In Sonnet 77, it is a sundial that marks time's passage, as the shadow cast by the dial's 'finger' moves round with the sun: 'Thou by thy dial's shady stealth mayst know / Time's thievish progress to eternity.' Shakespeare was familiar with the pocket or ring dial too, a portable device that had the hours of the day marked on the inside. When held up to the sun, light passed through a small hole in the ring and where it fell on the inside indicated the time. In *As You Like It*, Jacques recounts how the fool he meets in the forest carries one in his pocket, or 'poke': 'And then he drew a dial from his poke, / And looking on it with lack-lustre eye / Says very wisely, "It is ten o'clock."' A fine pocket dial was a sign of wealth. Even more impressive was the newly developed pocket watch. Malvolio, imagining himself master of the household in *Twelfth Night*, pictures such a status symbol for himself: 'I frown the while, and perchance wind up my watch...'

Most people, however, relied on a public clock to tell the time, with a bell chiming to indicate the hour. In *The Merry Wives of Windsor*, Falstaff hears that 'The Windsor bell hath struck twelve; the minute draws on.' In *Cymbeline*, Giacomo, hidden in Imogen's chamber, counts as the clock strikes: 'One, two, three. Time, time!' In *Richard II* King Richard, usurped by Bolingbroke, contemplates his demise in exquisite horological detail:

Richard II
5.5

Now, sir, the sounds that tell what hour it is
Are clamorous groans that strike upon my heart,
Which is the bell. So sighs, and tears, and groans
Show minutes, hours, and times. But my time
Runs posting on in Bolingbroke's proud joy,
While I stand fooling here, his jack of the clock.

Some clocks had complex mechanisms and extravagant features, and the 'jack of the clock' refers to an automaton, whose movements were governed by the clock. It is an apt image for the powerless king who realizes his own time is 'broke': 'I wasted time, and now doth time waste me.'

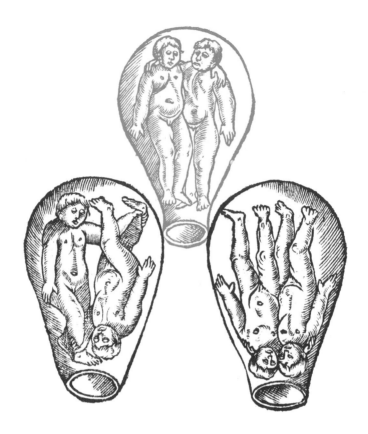

TWINS

❡ TWINS feature in two of Shakespeare's plays, *Twelfth Night* and *The Comedy of Errors*, both plays borrowing from Plautus's Roman comedy *Menaechmi* a storyline of separated twins. *The Comedy of Errors* is the more complicated for featuring two sets of identical twins, each pair sharing the same name. In the play, Egeon is searching for his twin sons, separated at sea. Both sons are now called Antipholus, and each is accompanied by a servant twin, both of whom are called Dromio. Egeon recalls how all four came into the world:

There had she not been long but she became
A joyful mother of two goodly sons;
And, which was strange, the one so like the other
As could not be distinguished but by names.
That very hour, and in the selfsame inn,
A mean-born woman was delivèred
Of such a burden male, twins both alike.
Those, for their parents were exceeding poor,
I bought, and brought up to attend my sons.

From the potential sorrow of separation, Shakespeare creates a comedy of mistaken identity. Antipholus of Syracuse, finally reunited with his brother, sums up their story: 'I was ta'en for him, and he for me, / And thereupon these errors are arose.' The servant twins Dromio of Ephesus and Syracuse, like their masters, are brought together in the final scene: 'We came into the world like brother and brother, / And now let's go hand in hand, not one before another.'

In *Twelfth Night*, Viola and her twin brother, Sebastian, are also separated in a shipwreck. Disguised in masculine attire in imitation of her brother, Viola is Sebastian's mirror image. When she is mistaken for Sebastian by his friend Antonio, she realizes her brother may still be alive: 'Prove true, imagination, O prove true, / That I, dear brother, be now ta'en for you!' When the twins are eventually reunited, Antonio is left to wonder: 'How have you made division of yourself? / An apple cleft in two is not more twin / Than these two creatures.'

Shakespeare's own twins, Hamnet and Judith, were baptized on 2 February 1585. Judith was to lose her twin brother just eleven years later, however. Hamnet died and was buried at Stratford-upon-Avon on 11 August 1596.

UNICORN

 ☞ ALTHOUGH DESCRIPTIONS varied in the sixteenth century, the legendary unicorn was generally agreed to be horse-like in appearance, with cloven hooves, and a single spiralled horn protruding from its forehead. A notoriously wild creature – Lucrece alludes to the time it takes 'to tame the unicorn' – it was said the unicorn could be tamed only by virgins and, by association, the beast became a symbol of purity. Edward Topsell includes the unicorn in his *History of Four-Footed Beasts...* alongside the hydra, sphinx and other mythical creatures. He describes how hunters would lure and tame the unicorn by dressing as maidens and how the lion might catch the unicorn by running for the trees, the unicorn pursuing it so quickly that it 'runneth against the tree, wherein his sharp horn sticketh fast'. Shakespeare alludes to this when it is said of Julius Caesar 'he loves to hear / That unicorns may be betrayed with trees', and in *Timon of Athens*, Timon says to Apemantus:

Tab: X

Monoceros Unicornu
Einhorn

Capricorn, Marin,
Meer Steinbock

Monoceros Unicornu.
Einhorn.

'Wert thou the unicorn, pride and wrath would confound thee, and make thine own self the conquest of thy fury.'

The unicorn was prized for its horn, which was believed to have magical properties. A German visitor to the court of Elizabeth I reported being shown what was claimed to be the horn of a unicorn, almost two metres in length, and valued at more than £10,000, a colossal sum at the time. Said to be able to detect poisons, substances believed to be unicorn horn were used to line the goblets of wary royals. Ground into a powder, they were prescribed as an antidote to poisoning and were regularly dispensed by apothecaries as a panacea – the hoof and horn of less exotic creatures providing a convincing substitute in the absence of the real thing. Indeed, any horn purported in Elizabethan England to be from a unicorn was most likely the horn of a narwhal. In 1577, the English explorer Martin Frobisher had discovered one of these intact in the ice in northern Canada and presented it to the Queen on his return as the horn of a sea-unicorn. As overseas exploration and sightings of living narwhals became more commonplace, however, the legend of the unicorn was met with increasing scepticism. In *The Tempest* it takes the apparition of strange spirits, conjured by Prospero, to convince Sebastian: 'A living drollery. Now I will believe / That there are unicorns.'

URCHIN

¶ URCHIN IS AN OLD-FASHIONED, and now rarely used, word for the hedgehog. Medieval bestiaries, books that illustrated real and imaginary beasts with accompanying moral text, depicted hedgehogs rolling in apples so that the fruit stuck to their prickles and could be carried away, an observation that first appeared in the writings of the Roman author Pliny the Elder. Although more

usually known as a hedgehog or hedgepig by Shakespeare's time, the strange stories around the creature's behaviour persisted. Writing in *The History of Four-Footed Beasts...* (1607), Edward Topsell also described hedgehogs rolling in apples, as well as worms and grapes. The hedgehog's nocturnal habits may additionally have inspired the belief that it stole the milk from sleeping cows.

In Shakespeare's plays the hedgehog is presented as a disagreeable creature. The fairies sing in *A Midsummer Night's Dream* to deter the 'spotted snakes' and 'thorny hedgehogs', and in *The Tempest* Caliban describes the spirits sent by Prospero to torment him as 'like hedgehogs, which lie tumbling in my barefoot way and mount their pricks at my footfall'. Urchin is also an obsolete word for a goblin or mischievous sprite, and earlier in the same speech Caliban complains that if Prospero bids them, the spirits will 'fright me with urchin-shows'.

URINAL

The Merry
Wives of
Windsor
3.1

I will knog your urinal about your knave's cogscomb.

¶ IN THE ELIZABETHAN CONTEXT, a urinal is a vessel for urine, used by physicians, who would examine patients' urine to diagnose the nature of their illness, a practice known as uroscopy or casting the water. It was believed that the smell, colour and clarity of the urine and the consistency of its crown, or top, were all aids to diagnosis. Physicians could compare the urine colour to a uroscopy colour wheel that indicated a specific disease for each of its twenty different colours. Hence, in *The Two Gentlemen of Verona*, Speed declares of the obviously lovesick Valentine: 'these follies are within you, and shine through you like the water in an urinal, that not an eye that sees you but is a physician to comment on your malady.'

By the seventeenth century, casting the water as a method of diagnosis had been rejected by many physicians, although Shakespeare's son-in-law, the physician John Hall, continued to examine patients' urine, recording in one patient's case notes in 1624 that 'his Urine was thin, red, the Crown yellow and frothy.'

VENICE

What news on the Rialto?

The
Merchant
of Venice
1.3

☞ VENICE IS A CITY on the northeast coast of Italy and the setting for two of Shakespeare's plays, *The Merchant of Venice* and *Othello*. In Shakespeare's time, Venice was an international hub for maritime trade, home to a multicultural population and to a prosperous merchant class that gravitated to the Rialto, the commercial heart of the city. In his book *Coryat's Crudities*, published in 1611, Thomas Coryat records that 'you may see many Polonians, Slavonians, Grecians, Turks, Jews, Christians of all the famousest regions of Christendom' in St Mark's piazza. For all the city's diversity, however, Jewish people were forced to live in a segregated area known as the Venetian Ghetto, and Shylock, a Jew, encounters anti-Semitism throughout *The Merchant of Venice*. Venetian society is prejudiced against Othello too. Roderigo tells Brabantio in the very first scene that he has seen his daughter Desdemona: 'Transported with no worse nor better guard / But with a knave of common hire, a gondolier, / To the gross clasps of a lascivious Moor...'

Roderigo's speech sets the play in a city renowned for its canals and its gondolas. In *The Merchant of Venice*, Lorenzo and Jessica are reportedly 'seen together' in one and, in *As You Like It*, commenting on Jaques's melancholy disposition from his travels, Rosalind tells him 'I will scarce think you have swam in a gondola.' Venice also had a reputation for decadence and was famed for its courtesans. Iago alludes to this in *Othello*, calling Cassio's lover Bianca 'a hussy that by selling her desires / Buys herself bread and cloth,' and he plays on the low reputation of Venetian wives in order to feed

Othello's jealousy: 'I know our country disposition well. / In Venice they do let God see the pranks / They dare not show their husbands...'

Coryat's Crudities paints a vivid, intoxicating picture of the Venetian courtesan's world, from their 'delectable adornments' to their palatial rooms 'most glorious and glittering to behold' – though Coryat is at pains to point out to the reader that he went there only 'to see whether these things were true'.

VICTUALS

The Comedy
of Errors

3.1

Small cheer and great welcome makes a merry feast.

❡ AN OLD WORD from Middle English, victuals refers to food and drink, provisions or supplies. A victualler by association is somebody who provides these, and in Shakespeare's time this would have included an innkeeper or tavern owner. In an alehouse, simple,

everyday food could be purchased, including bread, cheese, bacon, beans and pottage – a thick stew or soup made with vegetables, grains, meat or fish. Most ordinary Elizabethans would have eaten their breakfast at home, with some cold meat, bread and butter, and then perhaps had their midday meal in an inn. Falstaff, it would seem, eats most of his meals in a tavern in *Henry IV part 1*, relying on the hostess, Mistress Quickly, to serve him: 'Hostess, my breakfast, come!' Supper could be eaten at any time between 5 p.m. and 8 p.m., depending on your social standing; gentlemen and merchants typically ate later. In *The Merry Wives of Windsor*, Sir Hugh finishes his supper and looks forward to dessert: 'there's pippins and cheese to come.'

Banquets, elaborate affairs with numerous courses and dishes served all at once, were the preserve of the wealthy and royalty. Arranged around an impressive centrepiece – a swan, a peacock or a wild boar – wild birds, lobsters, porpoises and eel were enjoyed by diners, who then moved on to jellies, puddings, pastries and preserves. In *Titus Andronicus* a banquet is planned, one that Titus hopes 'may prove more stern and bloody than the Centaurs' Feast'. His unusual ingredient? The heads of the men who raped and maimed his daughter, baked in a pie:

Titus
Andronicus
5.3

> *Why, there they are, both bakèd in this pie,*
> *Whereof their mother daintily hath fed,*
> *Eating the flesh that she herself hath bred.*

138

VOLUMES

*Slender: I had rather than forty shillings I had
my book of songs and sonnets here...You have
not the book of riddles about you, have you?
Simple: Book of riddles! Why, did you not lend
it to Alice Shortcake upon All-hallowmas last...?*

The Merry
Wives of
Windsor
1.1

❡ ALTHOUGH THERE IS NO documentary evidence of the
books that Shakespeare owned, borrowed or lent, his works are
indebted to the volumes he knew and read, from the Classical
literature he studied at school to Slender's 'Book of Songs
and Sonnets' in *The Merry Wives of Windsor* – most likely
a copy of *Tottels Miscellany* (1557), said to be the first
published anthology of English poetry. Shakespeare
would have read the *Workes* of Geoffrey Chaucer
(1602). *The Two Noble Kinsmen* is a retelling of
his 'Knight's Tale', the play's Prologue acknow-
ledging that 'Chaucer, of all admired, the story
gives.' Similarly, *Pericles* is based on a story in
Confessio Amantis by Chaucer's contemporary
John Gower, and features Gower as the play's nar-
rator. Shakespeare mined Raphael Holinshed's
Chronicles (1577/87) for the plots of his history
plays. *Romeo and Juliet* is indebted to the narrative
poem *The Tragicall Historye of Romeus and Juliet*
(1562) by the English poet Arthur Brooke, whose
own work was inspired by an earlier Italian tale.
Shakespeare read books in translation too.
Ovid's *Metamorphoses* translated by Arthur Golding
(1567), Plutarch's *Lives of the Most Noble Grecians
and Romans* translated by Thomas North (1579),
and *The Essays of Michel de Montaigne* translated

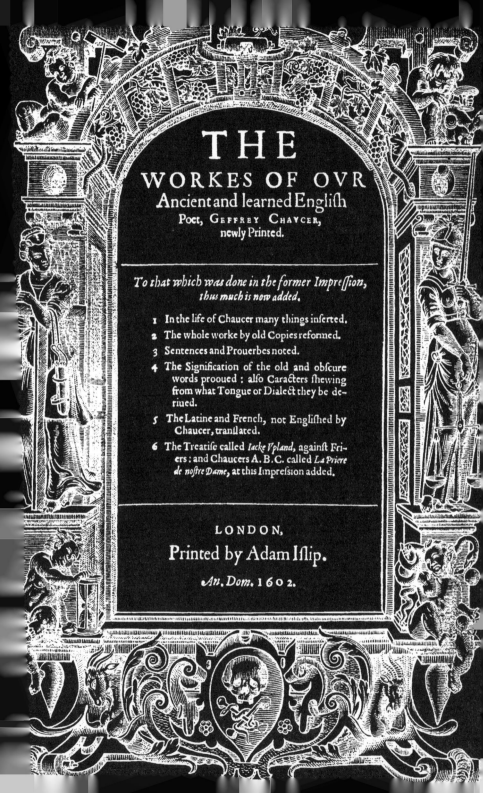

THE
WORKES OF OVR
Ancient and learned English
Poet, Geffrey Chavcer,
newly Printed.

To that which was done in the former Impreſſion,
thus much is now added.

1 In the life of Chaucer many things inſerted.

2 The whole worke by old Copies reformed.

3 Sentences and Prouerbes noted.

4 The Signification of the old and obſcure
words prooued : alſo Caracters ſhewing
from what Tongue or Dialect they be de-
riued.

5 The Latine and French, not Engliſhed by
Chaucer, tranſlated.

6 The Treatiſe called *Iacke Vpland*, againſt Fri-
ers : and Chaucers A. B. C. called *La Priere*
de noſtre Dame, at this Impreſſion added.

LONDON,
Printed by Adam Iſlip.

An. Dom. 1602.

by John Florio (1603) were all sources of inspiration. Montaigne's questioning essays helped to shape Hamlet's introspective character, and Montaigne's work 'Of The Cannibals' directly inspired Gonzalo's vision of the 'commonwealth' in *The Tempest*. In *Antony and Cleopatra*, the fantastical description of Antony's first sight of Cleopatra and 'the barge she sat in' borrows its imagery directly from North's translation of Plutarch. Comparison of these books with Shakespeare's plays suggests he must have had copies of them to hand when he was writing, so close at times are Shakespeare's lines to the originals.

At the beginning of his career, Shakespeare may have borrowed copies of the more expensive folio titles from fellow Stratfordian Richard Field, whose London printing house had printed Plutarch, for example. It is tempting to think, however, that, writing *The Tempest* towards the end of his career, Shakespeare has his own library in mind when Prospero says:

> *Knowing I loved my books, he furnished me*
> *From mine own library with volumes that*
> *I prize above my dukedom.*

The
Tempest
1.2

The power that is perceived to reside in books is evident throughout *The Tempest*. Caliban plots to seize Prospero's books, telling Stephano 'Remember / First to possess his books, for without them / He's but a sot as I am,' and as Prospero renounces his 'potent art' at the end of the play, he declares:

> *I'll break my staff,*
> *Bury it certain fathoms*
> *in the earth,*
> *And deeper than did ever*
> *plummet sound*
> *I'll drown my book.*

The
Tempest
5.1

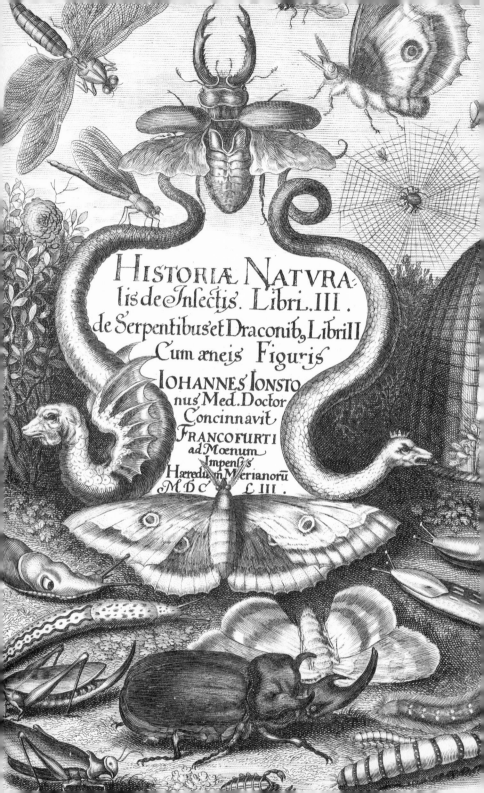

HISTORIAE NATVRA-
lis de Insectis. Libri. III.
de Serpentibus et Draconib, Libri II
Cum æneis Figuris
IOHANNES IONSTO
nus Med. Doctor
Concinnavit
FRANCOFVRTI
ad Mœnum
Impensis
Hæredum Merianorū
M DC L III.

WITCHES

All the charms
Of Sycorax, toads, beetles, bats,
   light on you...'

The
Tempest
1.2

☞ IN THE LATE SIXTEENTH
century, the belief that some people did the devil's bidding on earth was a powerful one. Curses, charms, conjuring spirits and black magic were all believed to be the work of witches, who were rumoured to be aided in this by their familiars, demonic spirits in animal form. In the *Discoverie of Witchcraft* (1584), Reginald Scot wrote that witches were usually old, deformed, pale and bleary-eyed, with lots of wrinkles. The label of 'witch' was almost exclusively applied to women, and carried a heavy penalty. Henry VIII had already made witchcraft a punishable offence and under Elizabeth I the 1563 Act Against Conjurations, Enchantments and Witchcrafts enforced the death penalty, burning or hanging, where harm had been proven.

Shakespeare mentions witches and witchcraft in several of his plays, most famously in *Macbeth*, where the Scottish King meets three prophesying witches on the heath in the opening scenes of

the play. Just as in Reginald Scot's account, these 'weird sisters' are withered and wild with 'skinny lips', and Banquo notes that they 'look not like th' inhabitants o' th' earth'. In *The Tempest* Prospero talks of the 'foul' and 'damned witch Sycorax', banished from her land 'for mischiefs manifold and sorceries terrible'. After capturing Joan la Pucelle (Joan of Arc) in *Henry VI part 1*, Richard Plantagenet taunts her: 'Damsel of France, I think I have you fast. / Unchain your spirits now with spelling charms, / And try if they can gain your liberty.' Joan, too, is described as an 'ugly witch'. In *The Merry Wives of Windsor*, Master Ford throws Falstaff (disguised as an old woman) out of his house. The moment is comic, yet highlights the very real fears and suspicions of many Elizabethans around magic:

The Merry
Wives of
Windsor
4.2

A witch, a quean, an old, cozening quean! Have I not forbid her my house? She comes of errands, does she? We are simple men; we do not know what's brought to pass under the profession of fortune-telling. She works by charms, by spells, by th' figure, and such daubery as this is, beyond our element. We know nothing. —
Come down, you witch, you hag, you!
Come down, I say!

WOOD

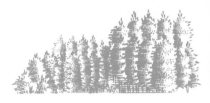

As You
Like It
1.1

*They say he is already in the forest of Ardenne, and a many
merry men with him; and there they live like the old Robin
Hood of England.*

¶ IN SHAKESPEARE'S TIME the Forest of Arden lay just to the
north of Stratford-upon-Avon and covered vast areas of land through
Warwickshire and into Staffordshire. His mother, Mary Arden,
took her family name from it and legend has it that the woodland
setting of Shakespeare's *As You Like It* was partly inspired by this
forest. Intriguingly, Shakespeare's source for the play, the prose
romance *Rosalynde* (1590), was set in the Ardenne forest in France.

The wood or the forest is traditionally associated with freedom,
magic, mischief and fertility, and Shakespeare imbues the action of
As You Like It and *A Midsummer Night's Dream* with these themes.
In both plays the characters hope to escape the harsh rules and
confines of their everyday lives by heading into the woods, and they
are changed by their experiences there. The banished Duke Senior
compares his old life with the freedom he now enjoys:

As You
Like It
2.1

*Now, my co-mates and brothers in exile,
Hath not old custom made this life more sweet
Than that of painted pomp? Are not these woods
More free from peril than the envious court?*

and in *A Midsummer Night's Dream*, Lysander suggests that Hermia defy her father by meeting with him in the woods to elope in secret:

A
Midsummer
Night's
Dream
1.1

> *Steal forth thy father's*
> *house tomorrow night,*
> *And in the wood, a league without the town,*
> *Where I did meet thee once*
> *with Helena*
> *To do observance to a morn of May,*
> *There will I stay for thee.*

Although it may be free from the constraints of the court and the city, the wood also poses its own threats and can be equally dangerous. In *Titus Andronicus*, Aaron encourages Chiron and Demetrius to use the wood for their villainy. The court, he tells them, is 'full of tongues, of eyes and ears, / The woods are ruthless, dreadful, deaf, and dull.' In *The Two Gentlemen of Verona*, Valentine prefers the 'shadowy desert, unfrequented woods' where he can sit all alone with his woes, and in *A Midsummer Night's Dream* a frustrated Demetrius warns Helena to stop questioning him, and to leave him alone: 'Or if thou follow me, do not believe / But I shall do thee mischief in the wood.' Wild and dangerous animals are found in the wood too. Orlando rescues his sleeping brother from a 'green and gilded serpent' and a lioness that 'lay crouching, head on ground, with catlike watch' in *As You Like It*; Theseus describes the 'lion, bear, or wolf, or bull' that Titania might see when she wakens in *A Midsummer Night's Dream*; and, in *Venus and Adonis*, Adonis is killed in the wood by a 'foul, grim, and urchin-snouted boar'.

X (CROSS)-GARTERED

Remember who commended
thy yellow stockings,
and wished to see thee
ever cross gartered.

☞ A GARTER was a ribbon or piece of fabric worn around the leg to hold up a stocking or a sock. In Tudor England, men in particular wore them over their hose (very close-fitting trousers), and colourful or elaborately tied garters were both practical and fashionable, drawing attention to the lower legs. Garters were also worn on ceremonial occasions by members of The Order of the Garter, an order of British chivalry founded in 1348 by King Edward III; its insignia was a blue garter or buckled strap with the motto *Honi soit qui mal y pense* ('shame on him who thinks ill of it') in gold lettering. As a small boy in 1495, Henry VIII was made a Knight of the Order by his father, King Henry VII. Contemporary accounts of Henry as a young man describe his athletic build and strong, muscular legs, and though Hans Holbein's famous portrait of 1536 depicts an older, stouter Henry, he still stands proud, displaying garters on both his legs.

In *Twelfth Night*, Shakespeare has the Countess Olivia's steward, Malvolio, proudly display gartered legs too. Tricked by other members of the household into appearing before Olivia in yellow stockings with crossed garters, the pompous Malvolio believes Olivia must be in love with him. The letter he thinks she wrote to him specifically commended his legs and his stockings, no matter, he says, that 'this does make some obstruction in the blood, this cross-gartering'. Unbeknownst to him, however, yellow is 'a colour she abhors, and cross-gartered, a fashion she detests', and his comically elaborate ensemble fails to impress.

YELLOW

*What beard were I best to play it
in?...I will discharge it in either your
straw-colour beard, your orange-tawny
beard, your purple-in-grain beard,
or your French-crown-colour beard,
your perfect yellow.*

☞ AMONG THE VARIOUS SHADES of yellow that Bottom
suggests for Pyramus's beard, the 'perfect yellow', he tells us, is a
golden hue, the colour of a gold coin. It is also the colour of Julia's
hair in *The Two Gentlemen of Verona*. Comparing herself to her rival,
Silvia, Julia observes: 'Her hair is auburn, mine is perfect yellow.'
Yellow hair was a sign of youthful beauty, and it was fashionable in
Shakespeare's time for wealthy women to colour their hair yellow
using natural dyes, such as saffron. 'Auburn' at this point denoted
a lighter yellow colour, faded and past its prime.

Yellow in the natural world also symbolizes the passage of
time. In *Love's Labour's Lost*, it heralds the springtime, when the
'cuckoo-buds of yellow hue / Do paint the meadows with delight'.
In the *Sonnets*, however, it is the colour of autumn, of 'yellow leaves',
and is symbolic of old age. Macbeth, sensing his own end is near,
observes that 'my way of life / Is fall'n into the sere, the yellow leaf,'
and in *Henry IV part 2* the Lord Chief Justice
lists 'a yellow cheek' among the physical
characteristics of ageing.

By its association with gold, yellow was
also the colour of avarice. In *Timon of Athens*,
when Timon's financial troubles have literally
brought him to his knees, digging for roots,
he discovers 'Yellow, glittering, precious gold',
although he is quick to reflect how the world

Ceres

Pomona

Lace dedi vobis omnes herbas sementantes semen. quæ sunt. Gen. 1. 29.

Excideret ne tibi diuini muneris Author,
Præsentem monstrat. quælibet herba Deum.

THE HERBALL OR GENERALL Historie of Plantes.

Gathered by Iohn Gerarde
of London Master in
CHIRVRGERIE

Very much
Enlarged and Amended by
Thomas Johnson
Citizen and Apothecarye
of LONDON

THEOPHRASTVS

DIOSCORIDES

London Printed by
Adam Islip Joice Norton
and Richard Whitakers
Anno 1633.

Io: Payne sculp:

turns by this 'yellow slave'. Yellow had further negative connotations too, symbolizing infidelity and treachery. In *Cymbeline*, Posthumus, believing his friend Giacomo has slept with his wife, calls him 'This yellow Giacomo', and in *All's Well That Ends Well* Lafeu describes Paroles' deceitfulness as 'villainous saffron' that would have made 'all the unbaked and doughy youth of a nation in his colour'.

In the sixteenth century, yellow was also commonly associated with jealousy. In *The Merry Wives of Windsor*, when Nim plots to reveal Falstaff's wooing of Ford's wife, it is to incite Ford's jealousy and 'possess him with yellowness'. In *The Winter's Tale*, Paulina assures a jealous Leontes that the baby Perdita is his daughter. The baby is clearly the 'copy of the father' but Paulina hopes it has not inherited Leontes' jealousy, and has ''mongst all colours / No yellow in't, lest she suspect, as he does, / Her children not her husband's.'

Elsewhere in the plays, however, jealousy is evoked through green imagery. For Portia in *The Merchant of Venice*, jealousy is 'green-eyed', for Iago in *Othello* it is a 'green-eyed monster'. Although the green association is not unique to Shakespeare, it is perhaps testament to the influence of Shakespeare's language that jealousy today is thought of in these terms rather than yellow.

YORICK

That skull had a tongue in it and could sing once.

Hamlet
5.1

❡ IN ONE OF THE BEST-KNOWN scenes from all Shakespeare, Hamlet is given a skull by a gravedigger, and as he takes it in his hands, he reflects: 'Alas, poor Yorick. I knew him, Horatio – a fellow of infinite jest, of most excellent fancy.' The skull belongs to the court jester of Hamlet's childhood, and as he studies it, he asks 'where be your gibes now, your gambols, your songs, your flashes of merriment that were wont to set the table on a roar?' As he fondly remembers the jester's antics, Hamlet recognizes, that in death, Yorick is now just exactly the same as any other man, his body simply dust and bones. The gravedigger too is unsentimental, singing of pickaxes and pits of clay as he digs, and throwing out the bones of the grave's previous occupants as he finds them:

A pickaxe and a spade, a spade,
For and a shrouding-sheet;
O, a pit of clay for to be made
For such a guest is meet.

Hamlet
5.1

Although this may seem unusual today, it was common in the sixteenth century for bones that were disturbed as new graves were dug to be removed and deposited in a charnel-house. Often built near to churches, charnel-houses first appeared in the medieval period and were more common in Europe, though there are English examples that were used right up until the Reformation

in the mid-sixteenth century. In *Romeo and Juliet*, Juliet pictures these chambers as places to make you tremble, as 'o'ercovered quite with dead men's rattling bones, with reeky shanks and yellow chapless skulls'. An equally fearful Macbeth starts to believe the charnel-houses and the graves are sending back their dead men. As the murdered Banquo's ghost appears before him, the guilty Macbeth wishes him back in the grave:

Macbeth
3.4

Let the earth hide thee.
Thy bones are marrowless, thy blood is cold.
Thou hast no speculation in those eyes
Which thou dost glare with.

Similarly, Hamlet, confronted with his father's ghost, struggles to understand why his father's 'canonized bones' have burst forth from their shroud, why his tomb 'hath oped his ponderous and marble jaws / To cast thee up again'.

ZEPHYR

👉 IN GREEK myth-
ology, Zephyrus is the west
wind, the bringer of spring and
light summer breezes. Typically warm
and mild, a soft, west wind is sometimes
described as a zephyr. In *Cymbeline*, Shakespeare pictures a zephyr
gently 'blowing below the violet, / Not wagging his sweet head',
and throughout the plays there are countless references to the wind.
Closely associated with travel, in *Pericles*, 'well-sailing ships and
bounteous winds have brought / This King to Tarsus,' and in *Hamlet*
Laertes is assured 'the wind sits in the shoulder of your sail'. In
A Midsummer Night's Dream, 'the sails conceive / And grow big-
bellied with the wanton wind', and Pistol is asked 'What wind blew
you hither?' in *Henry IV part 2*. Slander has spread 'on the posting
winds' in *Cymbeline*; in *Julius Caesar*, Portia hears a rumour 'and the
wind brings it from the Capitol'. In *The Tempest*, Prospero promises
Ariel that on his release he 'shalt be free / As mountain winds'.

The wind is changeable and inconstant too; Hamlet's madness
comes and goes as it changes: 'I am but mad north-north west; when
the wind is southerly, I know a hawk from a handsaw,' and in *Romeo
and Juliet*, Mercutio describes his 'vain fantasy' as insubstantial
'And more inconstant than the wind, who woos / Even now the frozen
bosom of the north, / And, being angered, puffs away from thence, /
Turning his face to the dew-dropping south.'

There are close links between emotional states and the weather.
Enobarbus reveals that Cleopatra's passions are so great 'we cannot
call her winds and waters sighs and tears; they are greater storms

and tempests than almanacs can report.' Claudio in *Measure for Measure* imagines his own death, and fears that his spirit will 'be imprisoned in the viewless winds, / And blown with restless violence round about / The pendent world...', and King Lear in his rage and grief calls upon all the elements to do their worst:

King Lear
3.2

> *Blow, winds, and crack your cheeks! Rage, blow,*
> *You cataracts and hurricanoes, spout*
> *Till you have drenched our steeples, drowned the cocks!*
> *You sulph'rous and thought-executing fires,*
> *Vaunt-couriers of oak-cleaving thunderbolts,*
> *Singe my white head; and thou all-shaking thunder,*
> *Strike flat the thick rotundity o'th' world,*
> *Crack nature's moulds, all germens spill at once*
> *That makes ingrateful man.*

ZODIAC

¶ ON THE ADVICE OF JOHN DEE (1527–1608/9), scholar, trusted advisor and astrologer to the court, Elizabeth I was crowned Queen of England on 15 January 1559. Dee studied astronomy, philosophy, navigation, divination and magic and, after making a careful study of her horoscope, he believed this date to be suitably auspicious. Although Elizabeth is said to have been a firm believer in astrology, other notable scholars of the period were less convinced. Sir Francis Bacon (1561–1626), statesman, philosopher and scientist, would later argue for knowledge acquired only through sound reasoning, observation and methodical study. Astrology, he felt, was full of superstition and, though not without its merits, would benefit from the application of logic and science. Despite the advances in science in the Tudor period, it remained a superstitious age, in which mathematics and astronomy could sit alongside alchemy and magic.

Pocket books, or almanacs, detailed the movement of the planets and named the governing zodiac sign for each month, some illustrating the relation of each sign to parts of the body and their effects. *Kalendar of Shepheardes* (1604) included an entry for each sign. As the sun enters the House of Libra on 24 September, the author writes that 'the man born under Libra shall be right mightily praised and honoured in the service of Captains,' the woman 'debonair and merry, rejoiced by her husband'. In *Much Ado About Nothing* Beatrice reveals she was 'born to speak all mirth and no matter', her mother having given birth to her when 'a star danced'. An astronomical clock installed in 1540 at Hampton Court Palace showed not only the time and the date but also the month, the moon phases, the movement of the sun and the signs of the zodiac. It is in this very practical sense that Claudio refers to the zodiac in *Measure for Measure* when he describes the crimes that have gone unpunished and that have been forgotten 'so long that fourteen zodiacs have gone round'.

Shakespeare's plays are rich in astronomical references, particularly to the stars. These are constant, guiding lights, fixed marks that allow men to navigate, find their bearings and mark time. In *Hamlet*, Barnardo describes the hour at which the Ghost appeared: 'When yon same star that's westward from the pole / Had made his course t'illume that part of heaven / Where now it burns,' and in *A Midsummer Night's Dream*, Helena envies Hermia's eyes resembling 'lodestars' that have so entranced Demetrius. 'Lodestar' is an archaic name for Polaris, the North star. Moments before his death in *Julius Caesar*, Caesar tells the assembled senators that his mind is made up, his word as 'constant as the Northern Star, / Of whose true fixed and resting quality / There is no fellow in the firmament'.

The stars were also believed to be responsible for fate and destiny. Hence Romeo and Juliet are 'star-crossed lovers', Sebastian in *Twelfth Night* believes 'My stars shine darkly over me,' Othello describes Desdemona as an 'ill-starred wench' and in *The Tempest* Prospero imagines his good fortune depends upon 'a most auspicious star'. Conversely, Cassius in *Julius Caesar* believes men should be masters of their own fate: 'the fault, dear Brutus, is not in our stars, / But in ourselves, that we are underlings,' and in *King Lear* Edmund, the illegitimate son of the Earl of Gloucester, is dismissive of his father's equating unsettling and unnatural events with the movement of the stars: 'we make guilty of our disasters the sun, the moon, and stars, as if we were villains on necessity, fools by heavenly compulsion, knaves, thieves and treachers by spherical predominance.' In a private letter to Ophelia, Hamlet too refers to the stars:

Hamlet
2.2

Doubt thou the stars are fire,
Doubt that the sun doth move,
Doubt truth to be a liar,
But never doubt I love.

SOURCE OF SHAKESPEARE QUOTATIONS

Wells, Stanley, Gary Taylor, John Jowett and William Mongomery (eds), *The Oxford Shakespeare: The Complete Works* (Oxford, 2005, 2nd edition)

SOURCES OF OTHER QUOTATIONS

'great whitish apple, full of sap or moisture...'
John Parkinson, *Theatrum Botanicum: The Theater of Plantes* (1640)

'dreadful, fierce...'
Edward Topsell, *The History of Four-Footed Beasts, Serpents and Insects* (1658 edition)

'the familiars of Witches do most ordinarily appear...'
Edward Topsell, *The History of Four-Footed Beasts, Serpents and Insects* (1658 edition)

'standing on the bank...'
Original inquest translated into English in Richard Savage and Edgar Fripp (ed.), *Minutes and Accounts of the Corporation of Stratford-Upon-Avon and other Records 1533–1620* (London, 1926)

'former flourishing...'; 'the chief of the world's seven wonders...'; 'divers strange and monstrous creatures...'; 'the more than wonderful crocodile...'
George Sandys, *Sandys Travailes* (London, 1652)

'who are the only windowes of the minde, both for joy and dread, and the most of our affections are openly knowne and seene through them, and they are ordained and made of purpose to lighten all the body...'
George Wateson, *A Rich Storehouse or Treasurie for the Diseased*, 1631 (7th edition)

'allured by the vain show of those things...'
Cited in Catherine Richardson, *Shakespeare and Material Culture* (Oxford University Press, 2011).

'Published according to the True Originall Copies'
First Folio, *Mr William Shakespeares Comedies, Histories, & Tragedies*, Frontispiece (1623)

'being thought at first but an idle smoke, and their eyes more attentive on the show...'
Letter from Sir Henry Wotton to Sir Edmund Bacon, 2 July 1613
Cited in Stanley Wells, *Shakespeare For All Time* (Macmillan, 2002)

'All the sea coast is hot...'
Abraham Ortelius, *His Epitome of The Theater of the World* (revised edition 1603)

'Freely to use and exercise the Art and Facultie of playing Comedies, Tragedies, Histories, Enterludes, Morals, Pastoralls, Stage Plaies and such others, like as these have alreadie studied or hereafter shall use or studie, as well for our Solace and Pleasure, when wee shall thincke good to see them, during our Pleasure...'
Cited in Amanda Mabillard, The Royal Patent Granted to Shakespeare's Acting Troupe
www.shakespeare-online.com/plays/macbeth/jamesroyalpatent.html

'grow plentifully in Italy and other hot regions, where they doe maintaine great woods and groves of them, that their Silke wormes may feed thereon...'
John Gerard, *The Herball or Generall historie of plantes* (1597)

'keep such a-chanting...'
John Case, *The Praise of Musicke* (1586)

'Hic incipit pestis (here begins the plague)'
Composite register of baptisms, marriages, and burials
SBT DR243/1

'This Figure, that thou here seest put...'
Ben Jonson's poem, 'To the Reader', in the First Folio (1623)

'to think that scenes, invented merely to be spoken, should be enforcively published to read...' John Marston, *The Malcontent* (1604), Preface
Cited in Amanda Mabillard, Shakespeare in Print. Shakespeare Online. 20 Aug. 2004
http://www.shakespeare-online.com/biography/shakespeareinprint.html >.

'partly because it is the Secretaries common hand, and partly also, because it is the onely vsuall hand of England, for dispatching of all manner of businesses for the most part...'
Martin Billingsley, *The Pens Excellencie or the Secretaries Delighte* (1618)
Cited in Susan Brock, 'Handwriting in Shakespeare's Time', SBT pamphlet, 2014

'Neverthelesse, I approve not those, who are ever in the Tennis Court like Nackets, and heat themselves so much, that they rather breed, then expel sicknes.'
James Cleland, *The Institution of a Young Noble Man* (1607)
Cited in Charles Kightly, *The Perpetual Almanack of Folklore* (Thames and Hudson, 1987)

it 'runneth against the tree, wherein his sharp horn sticketh fast...'
Edward Topsell, *The History of Four-Footed Beasts, Serpents and Insects* (1658 edition)

'his Urine was thin, red, the Crown yellow and frothy...'
John Hall, *Select Observations on English Bodies* (1679), transcribed in Joan Lane, *John Hall and His Patients* (SBT, 1996)

'you may see many Polonians, Slavonians, Grecians, Turks, Jews, Christians of all the famousest regions of Christendom...'; 'delectable adornments'; 'most glorious and glittering to behold...'; 'to see whether these things were true...'
Thomas Coryat, *Coryats Crudities* (1611)

'the man born under Libra shall be right mightily praised and honoured in the service of Captains...'
Kalendar of Shepheardes (1604)
Cited in Charles Kightly, *The Perpetual Almanack of Folklore* (Thames and Hudson, 1987)
Verified in http://downloads.it.ox.ac.uk/ota-public/tcp/Texts-HTML/free/A30/A30887.html

The Shakespeare Birthplace Trust's collections can be viewed online at collections.shakespeare.org.uk

SOURCES OF ILLUSTRATIONS
a=above, b=below, c=centre
All pictures from the Shakespeare Birthplace Trust.

Aelianus, Claudius, *The Tactiks of Aelian* (London, 1616). Pages 15c and b, 16, 17, 45a

Ascham, Roger, *The Scholemaster* (London, 1571). Pages 6 (initial letter), 67 (initial letter), 106a, 118 (initial letter)

Boorde, Andrew, *The Breviary of Healthe* (London, 1557). Pointing hand device (throughout) and pages 147 (initial letter), 153 (initial letter) and endpapers

Bullein, William, *Bulleins Bulwarke* (London, 1579). Pages 4, 10, 13, 28 (initial letter), 130 (initial letter), 135 (initial letter)

Bulwer, John, *Anthropometamorphosis* (London, 1653). Pages 28b, 57a and b

Bulwer, John, *Chirologia: or the Naturall Language of the Hand* (London, 1644). Pages 58 and 59a and b

Burton, Robert, *The Anatomy of Melancholy* (London, 1676). Page 147

Camden, William, *Britannia* (London, 1600). Pages 19 (initial letter) and 150

Case, John, *The Praise of Musicke* (Oxford, 1586). Page 112 (initial letter)

Chaucer, Geoffrey, *Workes* (London, 1602). Page 140

Clarke, Samuel, *A Generall Martyrologie* (London, 1651). Pages 37, 38, 41, 144a

Coryat, Thomas, *Coryats Crudities* (London, 1611). Pages 30a, 63a, 127, 135c and b

Day, Richard, *A Book of Christian Prayers* (London, 1581). Pages 19b, 75b, 85a, 86, 89b, 90, 91b, 105b, 106c, 116b, 119b, 129b, 139, 151a, c and b, 155, 156a

De Grey, Thomas, *The Compleat Horse-man, and Expert Ferrier* (London, 1670). Page 65

Drayton, Michael, *Poly-Olbion* (London, 1613). Pages 63b, 91a, 144b, 145a and c, 146a and c

Du Bartas, Guillaume de Salluste, *His Divine Weekes, and Workes* (London, 1633 edition). Pages 82c, 83c, 157a

Dugdale, William, *The Antiquities of Warwickshire* (London, 1656). Page 68b

First Folio, *Mr William Shakespeares Comedies, Histories, & Tragedies* (London, 1623). Pages 8, 49, 50, 93 (initial letter), 95a and b, 103, 104, 108b, 109a, 110

Gascoigne, George, *The Noble Art of Venerie* (London, 1611). Pages 22a, 43b, 137

Gerard, John, *The Herball or Generall historie of plantes* (London, 1633 edition). Pages 14b, 33a and b, 48, 60b, 61, 62, 68a, 69, 96, 97a and b, 112, 113a, 117, 122, 148a and b, 149, 152

The Grete Herball (London, 1529). Pages 32, 113b, 134, 138, back cover (a) and endpapers

Harington, John, *Orlando Furioso* (London, 1634). Pages 45b, 125a

Heywood, Thomas, *The Hierarchie of the Blessed Angells* (London, 1635). Pages 26–27

Hill, Thomas, *The Gardeners Labyrinth* (London, 1597). Pages 23 (initial letter) and 52c

Hoefnagel, Georg, *Londinium* map 1572–80. Pages 46–47, 80

Holinshed, Raphael, *The Chronicles of England, Scotlande, and Irelande* (London, 1577). Pages 30b, 76, 78b, 84c, 85b, 107b, 143b

Hondius, Jodocus, *Map of the Americas* (France, 1619 edition). Page 121

Hopton, Arthur, *A Concordancy of Yeares* (London, 1616). Page 156b

Jonstonus, Joannes, *Historiae Naturalis Volume 1: De Quadrupetibus* (Frankfurt, 1650). Pages 130a, 131, 132c, 143a

Jonstonus, Joannes, *Historiae Naturalis Volume 3: De Insectus* (Frankfurt, 1653). Page 70, 71, 72, 123, 142

King James I, *Orders for the Plague* (London, 1603). Page 102

Latham, Simon, *Latham's Falconry* (London, 1615). Pages 42, 43c, 44a and c

Lily, William, *A Short Introduction to Grammar* (London, 1732 edition). Pages 14a, 106b, 119br

Machiavelli, Niccolo, *The Arte of Warre* (London, 1588). Pages 43 (initial letter), 56c, 124 (initial letter)

Markham, Gervase, *Hungers Prevention: or, The Whole Art of Fowling by Water or Land* (London, 1655). Page 44b

Mascall, Leonard, *A Booke of the arte and manner how to plant* (London, 1592). Page 52 (marginal decoration), 53

Muffet, Thomas, *Theatrum Insectorum* (London, 1634). Page 20

Nordern, John, *The View of London Bridge from East to Weste* (London, 1597). Pages 31, 39, 79b

Ortelius, Abraham, *His Epitome of the Theater of the World* (London, 1603). Pages 34 and 66

Ovid, *Metamorphosis*, translated by Arthur Golding (London, 1603). Page 97 (initial letter)

Ovid, *Metamorphosis*, translated by George Sandys (London, 1632). Pages 98 and 99

Parkinson, John, *Paridisi in Sole Paradisus Terrestris* (London, 1629). Pages 28c, 77 (initial letter), 101 (initial letter), 115 and 116a

Parkinson, John, *Theatrum Botanicum: The Theater of Plantes* (London, 1640). Page 33 (initial letter), 59 (initial letter)

Peacham, Henry, *The Compleat Gentleman* (London, 1622). Page 2

Perkins, John, *The Laws of England* (London, 1567). Page 107 (initial letter)

Plat, Hugh, *Delightes for Ladies* (London, 1611). Pages 105a and 114

Pope, Alexander (ed.), *The Works of Mr. William Shakespear* (London, 1728). Pages 3 and 120

Queen Elizabeth I Warrant 1592 (SBT ER115). Page 108a

Sandys, George, *Sandys Travailes* (London, 1652). Pages 25, 35, 73 (initial letter)

Scot, Reginald, *A Perfite Platforme of a Hoppe Garden* (London, 1578). Page 22c

Seventeenth-century hornbook (SBT 2008-1). Page 118b

'Shakespeare Portraits and Miscellanies', collected by W. O. Hunt (1672). Pages 7, 9, 55, 75a

Theobald, Lewis (ed.), *The Works of Shakespeare* (London, 1752). Page 148 (initial letter)

Tomlinson, Richard, *A Medicinal Dispensatory* (London, 1657). Pages 11, 12, 141

Topsell, Edward, *The History of Four-Footed Beasts, Serpents and Insects* (London, 1658 edition). Pages 18a, 21, 24, 29a, c and b, 36, 64, 130b, 132a, 133, 146b

Wateson, George, *A Rich Storehouse, or Treasure for the Diseased* (London, 1631 edition). Page 40a

Willughby, Francis, *The Ornithology of Francis Willughby* (London, 1678). Pages 51b, 92, 100a and b

Wither, George, *A Collection of Emblemes, Ancient and Modern* (London, 1635). Pages 18, 23, 40, 51a, 54, 60a, 74, 77a and b, 78a and c, 81, 82a, 83, 111, 124a and b, 125b, 153a and b, 154a and b, 157b.

About the Shakespeare Birthplace Trust

The Shakespeare Birthplace Trust is the independent charity that cares for the world's greatest Shakespeare heritage sites in Stratford-upon-Avon, and promotes the enjoyment and understanding of Shakespeare's works, life and times all over the world.
Registered Charity Number 209302
www.shakespeare.org.uk

Acknowledgments

Compiled by Emma Mulveagh and Adam Sherratt.
With special thanks to Mareike Doleschal, Louisa Stott, Andrew Thomas and Dr Nick Walton at the Shakespeare Birthplace Trust, and Avni Patel, Lucy Smith and Roger Thorp at Thames & Hudson.

All images from the Shakespeare Birthplace Trust.
Photography by Andrew Thomas.